Transitions in Jungian Analysis

This deeply personal book contains essays and articles that portray the evolution of the author as a practicing Jungian analyst. Themes of illness, death, and violence are inherent within the chapters of this book. She uses metaphors from music to describe transitions, some involve literal death, and others are metaphorical.

The chapters of this book provide an engaging and readable review of life from one Jungian psychoanalyst, featuring essays on topics such as physical illness, film, music, video games, and her dog. The author covers problematic psychological and physical conditions, each of which, through exploration and inquiry, provides a transition to a new depth of understanding and a renewed sense of self. The book begins with the death of Power's Jungian analyst and the subsequent experiences when she began a "new analysis." She describes a "mysterious illness" that took her from being a classical musician to becoming a Jungian analyst. Other chapters include one on the nature of violence, another on the clinical issue of the "negative *coniunctio*" in the consulting room, and another on body symptoms and illness as "vanishing mediators" that take her from one status to another.

A personal and engaging read, this new collection by an experienced analyst will be of interest to Jungian analysts, clinicians in both analytical psychology and psychoanalysis, and those undertaking psychoanalytic training.

Pamela J. Power is a clinical psychologist and Jungian psychoanalyst living in Santa Monica, CA, USA. She is a member of the C. G. Jung Institute of Los Angeles, where she served as clinic director and director of training. She has lectured nationally and internationally in the field of analytical psychology on a variety of topics. She is also a member of the Inter-regional Society of Jungian Analysts, the International Association for Analytical Psychology, and the International Society for Psychology as the Discipline of Interiority.

Transitions in Jungian Analysis

Essays on Illness, Death and Violence

Pamela J. Power

R Routledge
Taylor & Francis Group

LONDON AND NEW YORK

Designed cover image: © Getty Images

First published 2024
by Routledge
4 Park Square, Milton Park, Abingdon, Oxon OX14 4RN

and by Routledge
605 Third Avenue, New York, NY 10158

Routledge is an imprint of the Taylor & Francis Group, an informa business

© 2024 Pamela J. Power

British Library Cataloguing-in-Publication Data
A catalogue record for this book is available from the British Library

Library of Congress Cataloging-in-Publication Data
Names: Power, Pamela J., author.
Title: Transitions in Jungian analysis : essays on illness, death and violence / Pamela J. Power.
Other titles: Essays. Selektions
Description: 1st Edition. | New York, NY : Routledge, 2024. | Includes bibliographical references and index.
Identifiers: LCCN 2023044495 (print) | LCCN 2023044496 (ebook) | ISBN 9781032561271 (hardback) | ISBN 9781032561257 (paperback) | ISBN 9781003434009 (ebook)
Subjects: LCSH: Jungian psychology. | Self. | Death—Psychological aspects. | Violence—Psychological aspects. | Diseases.
Classification: LCC BF173.J85 P679 2024 (print) | LCC BF173.J85 (ebook) | DDC 150.19/54—dc23/eng/20231205
LC record available at https://lccn.loc.gov/2023044495
LC ebook record available at https://lccn.loc.gov/2023044496

ISBN: 978-1-032-56127-1 (hbk)
ISBN: 978-1-032-56125-7 (pbk)
ISBN: 978-1-003-43400-9 (ebk)

DOI: 10.4324/9781003434009

Typeset in Times New Roman
by Apex CoVantage, LLC

Contents

Acknowledgments

Earlier versions of several chapters have previously been published in part or whole.

Chapter 1, "Death of the Analyst," was presented at the North American Society of Jungian Analysts National Conference in Chicago in 2005 and subsequently published in *The Journal of Jungian Theory and Practice*, 2005.

Chapter 2, "A New Dog-Image," was first published in *Psychological Perspectives*, 2004.

Chapter 3, "Violence and the Religious Instinct," was first published in *Psychological Perspectives*, 2011.

Chapter 4, "Fits and Seizures: Dog as Therapist to the Analyst," was presented at a meeting of the Inter-regional Society of Jungian Analysts in 2007 and subsequently published in *Psychological Perspectives*, 2022.

Chapter 5, "Negative *Coniunctio*: Envy and Sadomasochism in Analysis," was first published in *Shared Realities: Participation Mystique and Beyond*, Fisher King Press, edited by Mark Winborn, 2014.

Chapter 7, "Melancholia and Catastrophic Change: An Essay on the film *Melancholia*," was first published in *Spring Journal* 88, 2012.

Sources and Abbreviations

For frequently cited sources, the following abbreviations are used:

CW: Jung, C. G., *Collected Works*. 20 volumes. Ed. Herbert Read, Michael Fordham, Gerhard Adler, and William McGuire. Trans. R. F. C. Hull. Princeton: Princeton University Press, 1957–1979. Cited by volume and by paragraph number.

Letters: Jung, C. G., *Letters*. 2 vols. Ed. Gerhard Adler. Bollingen Series XCV: 2. Princeton: Princeton University Press, 1975. Cited by page number.

MDR: Jung, C. G., *Memories, Dreams, Reflections*. Rev. ed., Ed. Aniela Jaffé. Trans. Richard and Clara Winston. New York: Vintage Books, 1989. Cited by page number.

Introduction

Transitions in Jungian Analysis: Essays on Illness, Death and Violence

Spirit of Psychology

When I was a senior in high school, my boyfriend, a philosophy student at UCLA, gave me *The Undiscovered Self* by C. G. Jung. I didn't understand much of what Jung wrote, but the impact was powerful. I found something meaningful that remained so for many decades. After high school, I studied philosophy, formal logic, and mathematics before changing to music and eventually to psychology.

While an undergraduate major in music, I studied the history and forms of music. I found the transition between one period and another of compelling interest. We know what the music of the Baroque period sounds like with its characteristics such as continuous sound as differentiated from the Classical period with homophonic sound and the use of silence between chords. How could the music of the Baroque period be so different from that of the Classical, from a Bach concerto to a Mozart concerto? There were many composers who played a role in innovations that moved music along, many who have been forgotten except as honorable mentions in the history of music textbooks.

How does anything or anyone change from one form to another? The change I refer to is syntactical change rather than semantic change. In the former, syntax is defined by the elements, grammar, and rules that determine what belongs and how they work together. Semantic change is where the words, notes, or content change, but the syntax is the same. For example, a Mozart symphony has the same syntax as one written by Haydn.

One paradigm of syntactical change is that it results from the process of negation and sublation where one stage is negated, yet preserved, changed, and brought to a different level. For example, all the elements of Baroque music are preserved in Classical music, tonality, notes, and chords, yet it is a different organization of those elements. Baroque music is not dead but carries the "spirit" once inherent in that musical organization into a new organization, the Classical forms of music.

As a person moves from one period of life to another, there is something of the same process. The prior organization is not dead but lives a different life after a transition. The word "death" emphasizes the depth of experience that an individual can have. One suffers, one labors (as in the birthing process), and one dies into a

DOI: 10.4324/9781003434009-1

new consciousness, and if one is fortunate, this process happens many times over the course of one's life.

The chapters in this book describe several "transitions" that aren't just personal to this author but are also manifest in art, literature, and the clinical setting. I cloak my experiences in my chosen words, knowing that other paradigms might serve as well. Gradually, one comes to know something of the nature of the "spirit" that motivates and impels one. It is one's "truth." These chapters describe merely my truth, not *the* truth.

Each chapter stands independently, and they can be read in any order. Some were originally written many years ago, early in my career as a Jungian analyst, while others are more recent. I stand by my early work as part of the unfolding of my process. Chapter 1 describes the deeply personal experience of the death of my analyst with a concurrent cancer diagnosis and the beginning of a new analysis. Chapter 2 introduces my dog, a border collie named Beatrice, who became a "transformative agent" in the discovery of what is described as the "inferior function" in Jungian typology. Chapter 3 discusses my lifelong interest in the topic of violence and my struggles to come to terms with it in the collective and my own psyche. Chapter 4 returns to my dog Beatrice, who at age 2 developed idiopathic epilepsy. Her condition stimulated a long "active imagination" between her seizures and my lifelong "fits." Chapter 5 investigates the destructive aspects of the psyche that can emerge and co-opt a productive psychoanalytic experience and drive it into a pernicious and intractable "negative *coniunctio*." Chapter 6 discusses the phenomenon of "feeling development" under adverse circumstances in the fields of literature, music, and film, with a focus on the period around the 2016 presidential election in the USA. I differentiate between feeling values and feeling as emotion. Chapter 7 is an essay on the film *Melancholia* by Lars von Trier that offers multiple perspectives on the "depressive" personality and how different people and aspects of people deal with "catastrophic change." In Chapter 8 I reflect on my body symptoms and illnesses as "vanishing mediators" that facilitated the movement of my psychological syntax from one status to another. Chapter 9 describes my passionate involvement in video gaming and how it became a source of refuge and reflection during an emotionally tumultuous period of my life.

This is a book on and about Jungian psychology and how my relationship with it shifted and changed over the years. Nothing has grabbed me so strongly and enduringly as the works of Jung. His writings have been a framework for my life, especially his works on alchemy.

Many individuals have given me feedback, suggestions, and words of encouragement, and have thereby facilitated the writing of the chapters of this book. My apologies to those I have inadvertently omitted. My thanks and appreciation to Greg Mogenson, Jennifer Sandoval, Constance Crosby, JoAnn Culbert-Koehn, Fanny Brewster, and Norman Fogel.

This book is dedicated to B.
Pamela J. Power, PhD
August 2023

Chapter 1

Death of the Analyst

For many years I was in a Jungian analysis that impacted me deeply. I experienced the breadth and depth of Jungian psychology: the personal and archetypal layers of the psyche, the prospective and reductive approaches to psychic material, the religious function and the workings of the autonomous spirit, facility with alchemy, a number of religious and mythological systems, and an ability to recognize and live the symbolic life. This analysis was conducted with diligent and scrupulous attention to shadow material, animus problems, and the paradoxical relationship of ego to Self. Therefore, it was a surprise to me that despite this thorough and lengthy analysis, the death of my analyst felt abrupt and premature. It precipitated a period of inner turbulence and chaos that lasted for several years.

I was in analysis with my former analyst weekly, at times twice weekly; for the last several years, analytic sessions occurred every other week. I went to my regularly scheduled appointment in early May. My former analyst began the session by telling me he had been diagnosed with widespread metastatic cancer in the lungs. He told me that it was the bladder cancer he had lived with for over 20 years. He further informed me that the doctors gave him six to nine months to live. Hardly able to speak, he answered my unformed question: "I plan to continue to see you as long as I feel well enough."

When I returned two weeks later, he began by telling me that he was "going downhill fast" and that this would be our last session. At the end of the session, he invited me to contact him if I had any need or wish to do so. Almost two months to the day he was dead.

In the weeks before his dying, I was informed that he wanted me to speak at his funeral on a particular topic, so I began to prepare what I would say. In addition, a colleague and I agreed to organize the public memorial service to be held a month after the funeral. I made no contact with my dying analyst during those two months and heard about his decline indirectly.

Earlier that year, I noticed an enlarged lymph node in my neck under my chin that felt like a small marble. I brought it to the attention of my internist at my next annual physical. When I saw her in June, she didn't seem concerned about it but referred me to an ENT specialist who, when I saw him a few weeks later, prescribed a round of antibiotics to see if it had an effect on the enlarged lymph node.

DOI: 10.4324/9781003434009-2

When there was no change, he recommended I have an MRI (magnetic resonance imaging), which I did at the end of July. The MRI showed a "well encapsulated mass," from which my internist concluded it was a benign salivary gland tumor. The ENT, however, insisted on an excision biopsy of the entire node after a needle biopsy result proved inconclusive. He wanted to schedule the outpatient surgery immediately, but I told him I needed to wait until after mid-August when I would be finished with the memorial service for my former analyst. Sometime during this period, I noticed a second lumpy lymph node developing further up under my ear. Late in August I underwent surgery to excise the first lymph node.

At home waiting for the pathology report, I knew from my research that the suspicion was lymphoma and that there were many types. I was prepared for the call which told me it was low-grade, follicular mixed small and large cell lymphoma. My internist sent me for a CT (computed tomographic) scan of my entire body to see if there were other enlarged lymph nodes. There was no sign of anything else except those two nodes in my neck. The oncologist I consulted with wanted to do a bone marrow biopsy to determine if it contained abnormal cells; however, she said that her course of treatment would be to wait and watch and treat with oral chemotherapy or radiation only if the nodes became a problem. Low-grade lymphoma, considered non-curable, is treated as a chronic illness; people survive for many years even when it is diagnosed, as it usually is, as stage IV.

In my current emotional turmoil, I became a difficult patient. I refused the bone marrow biopsy at my next appointment. If there was bone marrow involvement, my staging, currently at stage I, would jump to stage IV. I became angry when I thought over her treatment plan, which did not consider newer treatments recently approved by the FDA. I fired her after two visits.

I was distraught, confused, and desperately missed my dead analyst. I felt he could help me find the larger psychological perspective I needed with this diagnosis. He had lived with his slow-growing cancer that was diagnosed in the early 1970s. I wanted to learn more about how he thought about his illness. After all, he lived 26 years after his initial diagnosis. I was full of regret that I had not asked him more about his condition and especially his attitude toward it. I felt very alone. My husband was helpful and sympathetic but left any decisions up to me. I told my adult children, who freaked out at the notion that their mother had cancer; I was very disturbed at their abrupt change in attitude toward me. Sentimental or patronizing—either way, I had become an objectified entity. I told two close friends who felt sorry for me and, of course, were glad it was me and not them. After that, I stopped telling anyone.

In December I consulted with another oncologist who had been on vacation in August. He brought up the remote possibility that I had genuine localized lymphoma; rare for my type, but that I should check it out. He referred me to his friend and colleague, a likable professor type, who gave me a thorough examination at the end of the year: no bone marrow involvement, confirmation of original pathology, no signs of other cancerous nodes, and no signs of it becoming more aggressive. He spoke vaguely of various options.

Early the next year, I gave notice that I would leave my part-time position as clinic director at our institute, a position for 13 years. I loved the job, but I wanted to have more time to myself, not be so busy, and not be so involved with the institute. Toward the end of June, as I carefully prepared to turn over my job, I realized how depressed I was. I felt stuck in grief over the loss of my analyst; I felt stuck in my physical condition, endlessly trying to make meaning of my situation and trying to find a way to move on. I was relieved to be leaving the clinic, but one more loss felt unbearable. I knew what I needed to do.

I called a colleague and said I wanted to see someone to process my grieving and that I wanted someone who was kind, had nothing to do with our institute, and had no prejudices about Jungians but mostly someone who would be able to give me space for the work I needed to do. I had in mind that I might see someone for a few months, no more. That was all I would need.

A few days later I received a name and made a phone call. After saying I was referred by so-and-so, we scheduled an hour for the following Monday. This was early July, almost one year after the death of my former analyst.

A New Analysis

I entered the consulting room of the new analyst with intense anxiety and hope. I poured out my story about the death of my former analyst, about the lymphoma, and about my disorientation. He didn't have much to say, nor did he ask me very much. Only when I described the beautiful metal vase that the interns gave me as a parting gift from the clinic did I break down in tears. Later I noticed that there was a crack in the backside. I explained to the new analyst that I felt like that vase: looked nice but had a big crack. I feared the nice analyst would think I was truly over the edge. He agreed to work with me but then told me that beginning the following week he would be on vacation for four weeks and we could begin after that in early August. I don't remember having any reaction to that announcement; instead, I left feeling some relief that he was open and not put off by my chaos and fragmentation.

During the early months of the new analysis, several phenomena occurred: first was the air conditioning.

During the summer months, and even into the fall, it seemed that this new analyst liked his consulting room on the cool side. The air conditioning in his office would frequently turn on and off. I was acutely aware of when it would do so and was extremely sensitive to the noise. When it would cycle on, it disrupted and interrupted whatever I was thinking or talking about. When I would stop and go silent, the analyst would ask what was going on. At first, I acknowledged that the AC had disturbed my process. Gradually I became openly angry about the AC. I informed the analyst that it was disturbingly loud and disruptive, and, besides that, his office was uncomfortably cold. He remarked that he didn't notice the sound of the AC. While my reasonable side understood that he had become habituated to the sound, I felt he was belittling me and accusing me of oversensitivity. I became worried that he thought I was using my annoyance at the AC as resistance or as a defensive maneuver.

He began to turn the AC off the first time I would react when it cycled on. I felt caught in a bind because I didn't want "special" treatment, which I felt it to be, yet the noise was intolerable. I stared at the AC vents up on the wall. I looked at them scornfully when the AC would cycle on, would feel great relief when it would finally go off, only to be anxious about when it would come on again. I informed the analyst that he had the cycling differential set too narrow, that it was set to a one-degree differential and he should set it to a two-degree differential so it wouldn't cycle on and off so frequently. He didn't seem to know what I was talking about. I couldn't help myself, nor did I want to; I became difficult, complaining, and constantly expressing my irritations.

Eventually, I accused him of being sadistic. I felt that he enjoyed seeing me in discomfort, enjoyed seeing the bind I was in. When he said the noise didn't bother him, I felt he was "gaslighting" me, that he was trying to drive me crazy. From this I concluded that he didn't like me, that he wanted to drive me crazy and out of his office, that he wanted me to quit, and that he was sorry he had taken me on.

Around the same time, I also complained about barking dogs belonging to my next-door neighbors. In reaction to that and to other material and from the few dreams I would share with him, he suggested that I needed an increase in the frequency of sessions. At this time, I was seeing him only on Mondays, and he frequently took Monday off when it fell on a holiday. I complained about this and compared him to my former gardener who came on Mondays but would not bother to show up or come another day when a holiday fell on Monday. I called him my "lousy gardener-analyst." I accused him of liking the benefits of being an analyst but not wanting to pay the price of being an analyst. I accused him of wanting me to come to more sessions just to make more money and that he enjoyed tormenting his analysands by coming and going as he pleased in a superior way. He suggested that I imagined he had arrived at a psychological state where things didn't bother him and that he didn't need to bother with feelings of helplessness, dependence, rage, or envy. He told me that perhaps I thought such a condition really existed and that I felt weak and inferior because I hadn't achieved this state. He implied, or I inferred from these conversations (which occurred numerous times), that I was wishing and longing for a state that didn't exist. I kept insisting that it did and gave him detailed descriptions of people I thought had achieved it. He said, "Do you think they don't pay a price for not being in touch with those feelings?" I challenged him: "Well, if they are paying a price, then they are blissfully unaware of it. And that sounds good to me!" He wondered out loud if I really *wanted* to pay that price and perhaps *that* was why I was sitting in his office.

Then the new analyst began to turn off the AC when I first entered the consulting room. I was furious because I hated the feeling that I had "pushed him into it." Yet, I was grateful for his response to my distress. I said to him, "You just can't win with me—if you do something, you are a bad analyst because you have acted out. If you don't do anything, you are cold and heartless and have no business being an analyst." To which he responded, "If my goal is to win, I certainly wouldn't be in *this* business."

When accusing him of sadism toward me, I could at times feel my own sadistic impulses, not toward him but toward my own analysands. I became aware of how much I would savor telling my analysands that I was dying and that "this would be their last session." What a pleasure to hurt and torment them so. I could hardly wait to become terminally ill so I could do so. The intensity of these feelings was deeply shocking and disturbing, but there was surprising relief in feeling them.

For many months I was buffeted between defensive contempt of my new analyst and the humiliation of being in analysis again. I hated my obvious neediness and the primitive states this analysis evoked—how crazy-making the situation was. I hated his dream interpretations, his limitations, his forgetfulness, and his seeming indifference toward me. I hated the whole thing.

When I was refractory or pressed him with my concerns or my complaints, I felt the risk of being rebuffed, of feeling humiliated, of being thought of as pathological, and I worried in general about whatever he might be thinking. But I felt as if my life was at stake, that I had no choice, and that urgent matters were pressing upon me.

Meanwhile, nothing was being done about my lymphoma. After two excision biopsies, the remaining portion of one lymph node was growing larger, but I was doing nothing. This was not unreasonable, as a "watchful waiting" protocol was and had been one of my options. I was aware that I was in conflict about any treatment, thinking about my former analyst, whom I knew had refused any radical treatment for his condition. In addition, there was an uncanny feeling of indifference regarding my condition. However, during the early months of my new analysis, I returned to my local oncologist, who became alarmed that I hadn't proceeded with some treatment, given the fact that all signs pointed to an unusual presentation of localized low-grade lymphoma. He got on the phone and spoke with the likable professor, and together they sent me to a radiation oncologist for a consultation. That visit produced a number of options. I chose limited radiation on my neck where the lymph node continued to grow. I received daily radiation for four weeks in the fall of that year.

At some point I realized how much attention I gave to my new analyst's physical and psychological health and well-being. I could sense with disturbing accuracy when he was not feeling well, something was on his mind, or he was distracted. When he had a cold, when he moved with more than his accustomed stiffness, the slight change in the tone of voice when something was going on—I noticed them all. Two issues that got the most attention were his back problems, which were evident from the way he sat, and his coughing. I put effort into helping him with his back problems, having been through my own back problems. I knew what he should do and not do. I was worried he would have back surgery and told him not to. I was distressed because I felt he would not take any of my advice seriously because it came from an analysand. His coughing I ignored, but it was the greater problem. Gradually I realized that I was extremely anxious about his coughing. Was he seriously ill?

During the final months and weeks with my former analyst, he did *not* cough. He had an inhaler and once mentioned casually that he had late-onset asthma. I took his word about that as well as the explanation for the large piece of cardboard taped over the vent high on the wall. He explained his theory that dust particles coming through the vent were causing an allergic asthmatic response. Only later did I understand that he was having trouble breathing because of lung cancer, not because of allergies. When my new analyst told me he suffered from allergies, I didn't believe him but didn't know why. I was sure it was something more serious and he wasn't telling me or taking his symptoms seriously. When I was aware of how anxious I was, I pressed him about his health. Eventually, he told me that he had been thoroughly checked out and there was no sign of anything serious. This issue led to numerous discussions over weeks about my concerns for his well-being. I insisted that they were entirely selfish, that I didn't want another analyst dying on me, that everyone seemed to die on me, and that I had no say-so about it. He remarked that we are all in that boat, even with ourselves, and how vulnerable we are about loved ones dying suddenly or slowly and how frightening it is and that, given my history, I am very sensitive and anxious in that area.

My History

Oh, yes, my history. I was born during WWII while my father was fighting in the European and North African campaigns. He returned when I was 2½. Then just after I turned six, my father contracted a strep infection that went to his kidneys, causing glomerulonephritis. He was hospitalized, and ten days later he died of a stroke secondary to the kidney infection. It was a sudden and unexpected death. No one thought he would die from his condition. The shock to my mother reverberated through the family. My older sister was aged eight, and my younger sister was just four months old. It was the custom in those days to protect children from the horrors of death. Children were not brought to the funeral; nor were we present at the second funeral held in another state the following week or at the graveside for the burial. I first visited my father's grave in Marblehead, Massachusetts, while on a trip to Boston, when my daughter was attending college.

I had no subsequent father figure until my first analysis, which began when I was aged 19. My second analysis, began at age 27, ended after four years with the illness and death of *that* analyst. My third analysis spanned almost 24 years, and given the length and depth of experience with him, I thought of him as the closest replacement to a father I had experienced.

Despite my former analyst's awareness and sensitivity, the replication of the death experience was uncanny. I kept myself unaware of how ill my former analyst was as I had been about my own father. As if following a very old script, I kept myself outside his dying process, not contacting him, not wanting to know, as if to know were going against an ancient taboo. On the other hand, I wonder how unaware I really was. I remember when my former analyst told me about his allergies and showed me the cardboard over the heating vent in his office: I had a powerful urge to bring him my portable air purifier. I was sure it would help his breathing problems. I squelched this strong impulse, sensing that it would not be well received, perhaps even be deemed a "presumptive intrusion." The day after my father died, I walked into my mother's bedroom wanting to have some contact with her to understand all the emotional turmoil that I felt in the house: something terrible had happened; what was it? I needed confirmation or something. I was met with an angry rebuff that told me to get away from her, that I was intruding upon her emotional state.

I was fortunate that my new analyst recognized and accepted my healing impulses toward him. He didn't buy my statement when I said, "It is purely selfish on my part—I want you to be alive for my needs." This had been said with denigration toward myself and a fear of vulnerability should I be in touch with the genuine concern it also carried. My new analyst suggested that there was human care and love in my concerns about his health and that I probably felt the same toward my dying father and my mother in her grief after my father died. Yes, one's own selfish need was involved but also an inborn capacity to love and care for another. This quality had rarely been acknowledged or mirrored to me, and I was very moved by his interpretations.

The Parked Cars

Early in my new analysis, I became annoyed by the analysands who came before and after me. There was one designated parking space available. I began to hate the man whose black car was in the parking spot for the hour before mine. I watched to see if he came out late or if he was slow to vacate the parking place. When it was two minutes before my session time, I would be furious if he had not vacated *my* spot so that I could park. I couldn't stand to see any other analysands around his house; I hid and became enraged if someone looked directly at me. I was shocked by the intensity of these "irrational" emotions.

During my former analysis, I regularly met and greeted the analysand who preceded me and the one who followed me. They were colleagues and friends, people I knew around the institute. All was pleasant and nice, and for years I accepted the situation, feeling well-analyzed and beyond any sibling rivalry. I was surprised that when given the opportunity, these murderous rivalries surfaced so powerfully. I would arrive at my session ready to discuss some matter I'd been thinking about all weekend only to "waste" half my session on my feelings about the man with the black car. He had gotten there first, and I couldn't stand it. But gradually I could stand it and came to accept lost and forbidden feelings about my older sister who had "gotten there first" because she had the best of my mother and father. They also carried unfelt feelings about the sibling analysands of my former analyst. And, lastly, they carried rivalry and envy toward my new analyst who, by having knowledge and understanding that was now helpful to me, had "gotten there first."

The Boiling Eggs

My new analyst would frequently interpret my complaints about him, about people who disappointed or frustrated me, as complaints about the breaks between sessions, weekend breaks, and especially breaks when he was gone on vacation. I dismissed these interpretations because, early on, I genuinely did not feel there was anything to them. I would become angry at him for what I called his "mechanical interpretations." One time, when he let me know he would be gone for one week, I responded that I would be glad for the extra time in my schedule. At this point, I was seeing him three times per week. The following weekend, I developed an upset stomach, and by Monday morning (when I usually see him), there were more symptoms of general gastrointestinal disturbance. The thought briefly crossed my mind that my malaise could have to do with his absence, but I brushed over the idea that he might be right and that my emotional, even physical, well-being could have anything to do with him. Later, however, I became tearful wondering how the baby or child "me" might have felt at the seemingly arbitrary absences of my mother and father. Later still, I became tearful at the loss of my former analyst, feeling how I longed to have discussions with him that I didn't have with him when he was alive and now, could never have. Feelings of regret, longing, loss, and love welled up in me.

My symptoms continued throughout the week, and I was aware of feeling anxious and on edge. I feared that my body symptoms were indications that my lymphoma had returned. My husband reminded me that I was currently under a lot of stress. But I felt like I couldn't and wouldn't survive and that my death was imminent. Malaise and lethargy came and went throughout the week.

One evening my husband put two eggs into a pot of water to hard-boil them for the tuna salad he was making. Standing in the kitchen, I heard slight but distinct high-pitched noises and wondered where the sounds were coming from. As I moved around, I discovered they were coming from the eggs in the water that was heating up. I couldn't believe my ears! They sounded like little chirps or peeps coming from inside the eggs. I had the reasonable thought that air was escaping from the eggs as they were heating up, but this thought was overwhelmed by an avalanche of panic and the feeling that there were live chickens in those eggs that were desperately chirping to be released. For a few seconds, I was utterly convinced that this was the case and was in a panic about what to do. When I voiced aloud my concern that there might be live chickens in those eggs, my husband stated calmly that they were *not* fertile eggs, having purchased them himself from the market a few days before. His statement did little to dissuade me from my momentary delusion. A few minutes later, I was able to resume my evening tasks. However, I kept an eye on the eggs, and when they were cooked and cooled down, I took one in hand and tapped it against the sink to see for myself.

The image of fully mature chickens trapped in eggshells screaming for help became the metaphor to understand my distress during the week: indifferent adults, not aware or able to hear my screams for help. My new analyst, absent, preoccupied with other matters that had nothing to do with me, was reminiscent of my preoccupied mother, my absent or dead father, and my former analyst who I assumed could not hear me or, if he did, would be so annoyed with me that he would dismiss me from his practice. Fears and anxieties of breaking out of my defensive shell and being born into a new world were powerful. I had been encapsulated in my former analysis, safe, but with parts of me unborn, unseen, and unheard. My anxiety and fear kept me there, and now there were anxieties and fear that I would never get out or, if I did, that I couldn't bear it.

The following week, when my new analyst returned to work, I expressed my fears concerning his absence, my fantasies that he was ill, was in the hospital, or had died or that he would tell me he had been diagnosed with a critical illness. I was able to feel my current anxiety linked to feelings surrounding my former analyst's illness and death, as well, as to my own father's illness and death.

Idealizing Transference

An idealizing transference toward my former analyst protected and defended me against a number of difficult emotions that, if I had been able to feel, might have better prepared me for his death and the feeling of abrupt termination. Looking back, I recognize repeated attempts on *his part* to let me know himself as fully human, someone with flaws and limitations, in order to break down my self-protective idealization. However, I was very resistant to that process, needing instead for him to remain bigger than life and for me to be connected to my own realized self through him. I felt special to my former analyst and basked in that perception.

My new analyst seemed flawed and limited from the beginning. I was disturbed and at times quite disoriented when he could not remember facts I had told him from one session to the next. I compared this experience to the razor-sharp precision of my former analyst, who never forgot a detail, or a dream, and who was or seemed to be completely reliable. My new analyst seemed deficient when it came to dream interpretation. I did not trust him with dreams from the outset and did not reveal much dream material out of fear of his misunderstanding or misinterpretation. My former analyst could pull profound meaning from the most paltry dream fragment. Who could top that?! Worst of all was the excruciating feeling with my new analyst that I was a forgettable analysand, not very interesting, not special, and not worth remembering from one session to the next. I felt lost and unimportant in his big analytic practice.

I knew in my head that I was experiencing the gradual dismantling of my previous idealization and the concomitant need to devalue my new analyst. But in my emotional life, these discrepancies were disturbing, disorienting, and painful. There were times I wanted to run away in humiliation or rage, but gradually I became able to tolerate the situation. I began to feel relief that I was NOT special, that my new analyst could be helpful and a disappointment, and that I could feel these feelings, and even be grateful for them.

The Conflict

After I had been in my new analysis for several months, I confided to a friend, also a Jungian analyst, that I was in analysis with a non-Jungian psychoanalyst. He expressed his shocked reaction by telling me he thought it was repugnant. This friend became an outer mouthpiece for an internal animus voice expressing repugnance that I had betrayed the purity of my Jungian roots, had betrayed and been disloyal to my former analyst (this friend had been in analysis with him), and had gone the way of many who have taken on the methods and ideas of so-called personalistic psychologies.

This conflict was not new. I have been interested in and studied psychoanalytic writings since graduate school, where they have been very influential in forming my clinical perspective and approach. My former analyst and I would occasionally get into a dispute during which I would accuse him of not being able to understand certain psychological states I would encounter, particularly what I called my "black holes" of depression. I exclaimed to him, "But your experience was fundamentally different from mine; you had a positive mother and father experience, whereas I had a negative mother experience and zero father experience!" My former analyst would respond that I gave too much weight to causal explanations; nevertheless, he continued to tolerate and even encourage my interest and explorations of other schools of psychology.

I was extremely upset and confused by an interview given by my former analyst only weeks before his death[1] wherein my former analyst stated that he was discouraged and perplexed as to why so many people who had had a Jungian analysis would turn to psychoanalytic writings. The interviewer pressed on him that many found it helpful in their clinical work. But my former analyst dismissed it as if "Well, if you don't find Jung enough." I felt guilty and that I was a failure to be one of those who "didn't find Jung enough." At times my conflict was intense and painful and felt like a conflict of loyalties between my former analyst and the urgency to discover new ways of understanding myself.

My Training Institute

Following the death of my former analyst and during the time of these events, my training institute went through lengthy, acrimonious "divorce proceedings" (as they were referred to by some because of the attorneys involved on both sides).

In the immediate aftermath of the "divorce," the sentiment, especially among candidates, was that the institute elders could not "hold the opposites," and that the split was a failure of the ability to contain internal tensions and differences. With a range of opinions in between, the sentiment at the other end of the spectrum could best be described as one of celebrating a healthy mitosis.

My internal state, already in painful confusion, was exacerbated by these events. I had been professionally active at the institute for many years, but with the death of my analyst, things gradually came to a halt. I was no longer interested in teaching or being involved with the institute; I resisted because inside myself I didn't know what the hell I thought or believed anymore. My analytic practice did not suffer as I was, for the most part, able to find my bearings during each hour. Moving on and beyond my former analyst was accompanied by grief and a worrisome sense of betrayal.

Much as I did, following the death of my former analyst, my training institute became depressed, shut down, nonproductive, and uncreative. A great deal of psychic energy was taken up in dealing with tensions and factional disputes. Committee functioning got bogged down in stalemates or open conflicts. When it was announced that there was a group who wanted to leave and form their own training organization, shock, open hostility, and confusion within the general membership ensued.

From the perspective of the institute, those relatively few members felt like malignant tumors acting destructively toward the body of the institute. From the perspective of the departing members, the institute was felt to be a restrictive and inhospitable environment in which they were unable to be productive and creative in a way meaningful to them. In my imagination, they felt much like my chickens trapped in their eggs. The departing group felt that the institute resisted letting them go. Some at the institute felt they couldn't see the last of those folks quickly enough, while others grieved deeply over the loss. In the midst of this chaos, one could not know if indeed something wonderful or terrible was happening.

A few years later, the separated group was content and prosperous, and my institute found a renewed sense of creativity and vitality. It seems an inescapable conclusion that the divorce was beneficial for everyone involved despite the traumatic process and resulting hurt feelings all around.

Somatic Symptoms

The timing of my lymphoma diagnosis with the death of my former analyst was remarkable. Some ways that I have pondered the coincidence include the following: my psyche knew that he was ill and dying before it was a known fact to me. My illness was in part an attempt to take on his illness and cure him and in part an attempt to live my loyalty to him so fully that I would follow him into death. My growth and development became encapsulated because it could not become conscious or integrated *at that time*. As my anxiety about being separated from him grew, genuine expressions got split off into the body. Once upon a time, I felt free to "have it out with him" about some issue or get into an argument or disagreement over something he said. At those times I found him remarkably open and receptive toward my feelings and my viewpoint. In the last many months, whether I felt *he* was less open or *I* was more fearful (probably both), I did not engage parts of myself freely. These unfelt feelings, "unthought" thoughts, not just unexpressed but kept unconscious, yet needing to be conscious, needing to be born, grew in my body as "well-encapsulated masses."

Whatever coincidence, causal link, or synchronicity connects my lymphoma to the death of my former analyst within weeks of each other, it brought about a necessary catastrophe, a conflict between life and death. In the midst of this process, I did not know what was happening to me—was it something terrible or something wonderful? I had no choice but to bring all my unsorted, disillusioned chaos into a new analysis. Out of this chaos and confusion, the lumpy, hard cancerous lymph nodes became eggs containing new life potential in need of being born. Daring to hear and feel the screams of desperation within myself cracked the shells and initiated a painful but creative process of a new psychological birth.

Prior to my new analysis, I knew *about* the primitive and infantile parts of my psyche, but I had not experienced them in the way I needed to grow and develop a fuller sense of wholeness. I could not access that development without a facilitating analytic container. I needed to enter into my black holes of depression, back to the desperation and despair of my early childhood to relive, repair, and reconnect. I needed to follow the autonomous spirit, the very core nature of the Self that will push aside loyalties or ideologies, if necessary, to find renewal.

The many years of my former analysis were an experience of the big picture about me, my inner world, and the outer world, and of me in those worlds. I draw on that experience every day for both my clinical practice and the practice of living my life.

My new analysis brought a microscopic view and experience of my psyche, with attention to the smallest details of my emotional life. I learned to connect the day-by-day and minute-by-minute flow of my psychic process. I learned to feel, experience, tolerate, and think about my unbearable emotional states, and I learned to grow and develop from the most primitive, embarrassing, and obscure parts of myself.

For some time, I used the analogy that my former analysis was an experience of *general relativity theory*, and my new analysis was an experience in *quantum mechanics*. At first, they felt incompatible and that the two could not exist in the same universe of my psyche, but gradually they did, and now they do.

Seven years after my former analyst died, I spoke about my experiences to a group of Jungian analysts and described how I had achieved a new sense of grounding and integration within myself. At that point, there had been no recurrence of lymphoma.

The End of Analysis

I continually found my new analysis useful, particularly in helping me recognize self-destructive tendencies such as the strange phenomenon of self-envy. When writing a paper or giving a presentation, he would point out when I would shroud myself, back off from my ideas, or attack my productions, as when an animal mother predates her own offspring. At first, I couldn't feel the self-envy as it was as difficult to feel as envy itself. At first, one can only notice the effects or results. I would write a paper and then dismiss it as "nothing" or nothing worthwhile. He told me that women wear burkas not just in Muslim countries. Women everywhere are forced to wear a burka, even to put on the burka themselves.

This tendency to "keep myself small and below the radar" and to protect myself from envious attacks (mostly from myself!) extended to travel outside the USA. I told myself that I would travel later in life when time and money allowed, but it was a version of constricting myself. When I consulted my first oncologist, she suggested I get going with whatever I wanted to do in my life and not postpone, given the uncertainty and unpredictability of my type of cancer. I traveled to England for a conference and then a year later to Italy for another conference where I gave a paper. Europe became manageable. When I was invited to go with a friend to a more exotic, unknown country, I found myself intensely conflicted. However, I bought tickets, got the required vaccines, and was prepared to go. Just a few weeks before my departure, I noticed a lump under my left arm. It was my pattern over the years to occasionally check myself for lumps that could indicate a return of lymphoma. It was small and I had to reach deep into my left armpit to palpate it. That hard lumpy feeling was unmistakable! I was sure this would kill my trip, and I could feel the relief at being "forced" to stay home. By the time I went to see my oncologist, however, something else kicked in. I wanted to do anything necessary to be able to go. My doctor thought it was a recurrence of lymphoma, but it was the axillary or sentinel node and when that node is enlarged it can indicate other types of cancer such as lung or breast. In addition, he wondered if the enlarged node might be a reaction to one of the vaccines I received. He scheduled a body scan and a biopsy. It turned out to be one isolated lymphoma that could be dealt with upon my return. I was elated and had a wonderful, and mind-expanding, life-changing adventure. After I returned, the lymph node continued to get bigger, so I consulted with my radiation oncologist again. "Oh, we treat that kind of lymphoma very differently now than when I treated you ten years ago." "Boom-boom" treatment, he called it, something he learned from "those smart guys at Stanford." After careful measurements and calibrations, I had two treatments of radiation on my now golf ball size axillary node. It shrank within two weeks and has not grown back. After 14 years, there has been no sign of a lymphoma recurrence.

My psychological understanding of that recurrence had to do with my continuing tendency to keep myself "well encapsulated," as the type of lymphoma was originally described. In addition, I had come to know that my "new analyst" loved to travel and would speak about places he had been if I asked him. The freedom he gave himself to go anywhere impacted me. He wanted to travel even when his health prohibited it. He hated being "grounded" as much as he loved the work of psychoanalysis.

A conflict that was never resolved between us was my irritation about the way he dealt with his patients before and after me. He frequently would run over time with his previous patient. There was a narrow walkway that made running into the person before me a continual possibility. When he ran over time, he expected me to ring the bell to signal him and let him know I was there. I didn't feel it was my responsibility and told him so. He understood my reactions only in a way that fit his psychoanalytic ideas of why I couldn't accept his dealing with patients before me. It was a conflict that we revisited from time to time. It was always my resistance and lack of acceptance of the analytic frame—his analytic frame! It was envy or sibling rivalry, or it was my lack of understanding and tolerance of his difficulties with time. That the analytic hour was something of a "sacred" rite was something my former Jungian analyst understood very well. My psychoanalyst and I frequently revisited the issue and ground away at each other over our differences. It might even be true that my attitude was a remnant of resistance and of my continuing desire to have *this* analysis be something of what I had with my former analyst. But the psychoanalyst remained utterly loyal to his analytic values as I remained loyal to mine. In the end, I was surprised at how useful it was to be able to grow psychological muscle for being seen and interpreted in a negative light *and* for him never to understand my perspective. Instead of simply learning to tolerate each other's differences, this felt like a significant achievement and a piece of unexpected psychological growth. I had come to accept his view of things many times, but this one I couldn't. In this one place, I strongly felt the difference between Jungian analysis and Freudian psychoanalysis. I came down on the side of being a Jungian.

An ongoing annoying habit of my psychoanalyst was his constant mentioning of "the end"—the end of the session, the end of the week, the end of life, the time of vacation, and breaks in the treatment. At first, I thought he had a case of "the ends" that needed ending and I told him so. But I began to feel that I wasn't allowing myself to consciously feel those endings and how they affected me. My defenses against attachment were strongly entrenched. My defenses against death were even more so. The sudden death of someone near me induced a dissociative state, deer in the headlight, a "no feeling state." Frozen emotional states in the face of death gradually began to thaw, and the new psychoanalyst would frequently speak of death and how unexpected, sudden, and frightening it can be. Given that he was several years my senior, he would remark that most likely he would die before me and that we were both dying. I remember deliberating about whether to "get out of Dodge" before that happened—again, but at some point, I made the deliberate commitment to stick with him until one of us was forced into an ending. We spoke about it frequently, especially when he had an ailment, back surgery, or treatment for cancer. I was able to do with him what I had not been able to do with my former analyst, my analyst before him, and, of course, with my father. He freely spoke about how he felt about aging, death, dying, and whatever was going on with him. I shared my responses, my fears, and my discomfort and growing ease with these discussions. Later in our work, he spoke about his analysis with Wilfred Bion and how he was surprised that Bion spoke frequently about death and dying. He, too, was taken aback at first by these conversations but then realized how useful they had been. Not talking about endings and death can keep one suspended in the pleroma, in the realm of infinity where mortality and the seriousness of death do not exist. That was where I had kept myself in the analysis with my Jungian analyst. I knew of his illnesses, and he spoke to me about his recurring treatments for his bladder cancer. Nevertheless, I found a way to live in a state in which he would never die and therefore I would never fully live in the earthly reality of my life.

Still, it was jarring and disturbing to receive a call that my "new" analyst, after seeing him for nearly 20 years, was in the hospital and another call a few days later that he had passed away. I had seen him for the last time only two weeks before his death. He loved analytic work and never wanted to "retire" so long as he felt his mind and body were "up to the job." During those last few years, I never felt a session with him was not valuable and worthwhile.

"Nameless dread" is what a child lives with when she has had a mother unable to metabolize the fears and anxieties of the infant.[2] The absence and then sudden and traumatic death of my father was an intrusion that haunted and distorted the relationships within my family and all my relationships in general. My mother, awash in her worries and depression during my infancy, was emotionally unavailable. The works with my Jungian analyst and my psychoanalyst gradually, and in their own ways, have metabolized the "nameless dread" I lived with since my earliest childhood.

There was no replacing my Jungian analyst with my psychoanalyst. One made me ready and receptive to the other. It might have even worked the other way around. Both were powerfully mutative and profoundly helpful.

Notes

1 Lawrence Jaffe, "Interview with Edward Edinger," *Journal of Jungian Theory and Practice* 1 (Fall 1999).
2 Wilfred R. Bion, *Second Thoughts: Selected Papers on Psycho-Analysis* (New York: J. Aronson, 1984), 116.

Chapter 2

A New Dog-Image

After my mother died at age 83 from a long, difficult, and unpredictable illness, I was exhausted from the months of caring for her and dealing with the dynamics of my extended family. I entered a period of withdrawal to grieve and recuperate. I could feel that changes were underway during this time, and I had no choice but to follow the currents.

> *Marie-Louise von Franz*: Every time one feels he has acquired a certain inner balance, a firm standpoint, something happens from within or without to throw it over again. This force always comes through the fourth door, which cannot be shut. . . . There one has to succumb, one has to suffer defeat in order to develop further. . . . The inferior function is the ever-bleeding wound of the conscious personality, but through it the unconscious can always come in and so enlarge consciousness and bring forth a new attitude.[1]

Months went by and Thanksgiving arrived. I went to a morning yoga class and returned home. Drying my hair after showering, I pulled out the newspaper that I had perused earlier that morning, picked up the phone, and dialed a phone number. Surprised when an actual person answered, I said, "I'm calling about the dog you have in the paper."

"It's an 11-month-old female, and she is spayed and trained." Eleven months—and trained! I couldn't believe my ears.

"When can I see her?" I calmly asked.
"Well, I'll be here for a couple of hours."
"I'll be there in 30 minutes," I replied.

> *von Franz*: inferior feeling has the advantage that there is really no calculation in it. The ego has nothing to do with it. . . . What touches people in the feeling of domestic animals is just this lack of calculation.[2]

She had short, brown and white hair. She didn't look like the pictures of border collies in my dog books. I liked her brother better. He also was brown and white,

DOI: 10.4324/9781003434009-3

but his fur was long, and he looked like he was supposed to look. He seemed more interested in me and wanted to play. His name was Buddy, but Buddy was, to all appearances, solidly attached to his owner and would not be going home with me. Mini-B, as the available female was called, seemed shy, uninterested in me, and uninterested in general. She had been sold as a puppy but recently returned to the breeder for unclear reasons. "You can take her home and see how you like her." I was surprised—he didn't even know me. I felt suspicious and a little hustled. I was about to say, "No, I'll think about it," when I heard myself say, "OK." We worked out the arrangements, and soon Mini-B was in a traveling crate with food and a leash in the back seat of my car.

> *von Franz*: When someone tries to meet his inferior function and experiences emotional shock or pain in confronting its real reactions, then the superior function, . . . like an eagle seizing a mouse, tries to get hold of the inferior function and bring it over into the realm of the main function.[3]

It wasn't that I hadn't thought about a dog. I had, off and on, since my previous dog had died of old age 5 years ago. I had been busy dealing with my mother's illness, and in the back of my mind, I was thinking that making another 15-year commitment at my age was out of the question. Nevertheless, a longing remained and pulled at me. Now, I wondered if a dog might bring some new life energy.

> *James Hillman*: The effort of maintaining consciousness with a function which is not primary is often too demanding. . . . An inferior function requires a disproportionate amount of energy.[4]

Whenever I thought about a dog, my pragmatic and reasonable thinking side got into an argument with my inferior feeling side. Thinking side: No more dogs! They are so much work and take so much time. Feeling side: Yes, Yes! A dog, a dog! Let's get a dog! Thinking side: You need to get a *symbolic* dog, not a real dog. Feeling side (wailing): You can't hug a symbolic dog; you can't play ball with a symbolic dog; you can't take a symbolic dog for a walk! Let's go to the animal shelter and find a nice dog that needs a good home. Thinking side: If you must get a dog, then do careful research on breeds and make a correct decision as to which one would be most compatible with your lifestyle. And don't forget, border collies are definitely out. They may be smart, but they are high-energy dogs and, really, you are too old and busy to take that on. Feeling side: Border collie! That's the dog we want!

> *von Franz*: An introvert who wants to assimilate his inferior function must relate to outer objects, bearing in mind that they are symbolic. He must not, however, draw the conclusion that they are *only* symbolic.[5]

At home, Mini-B was anxious, overly submissive, and shy. On walks in the neighborhood, she got spooked by people and baby strollers, in response to which she would cringe away or bark furiously. Gardeners with hoses, mowers, and blowers would send her into a fit of barking. She was aggressive toward anyone entering my house, would chase one of the cats in the backyard, or would cringe in the corner when chased by the other one. I was thrown into feelings of doubt and buyer's remorse. I could have returned her for at least several days, and on several occasions I almost did.

She had gone through the trauma of being taken away from her first home of nearly ten months. I had raised my previous dog from a puppy.

I was flummoxed by the situation: I did not know what to make of this dog nor did she of me. We were quite a pair.

> *von Franz*: The introverted thinking type's feeling has . . . very black and white judgments, either Yes or No, love or hate. His feeling can be very easily poisoned by other people and by the collective atmosphere.[6]

I hired an animal behaviorist/trainer recommended by my vet for private training sessions in basic obedience, believing this would help me and B with the bonding process. Instead, the problems increased. She was fearful of the trainer, crawled under a chair, and was unresponsive despite enticing chicken liver treats. Outside, B was so distracted that she was unable to focus on the simplest training exercises. Inside the house, with the trainer gone, she was sweet and compliant. I remained perplexed by B's behavior. After a few similar sessions, trainer #1 concluded that B had serious problems, perhaps stemming from abuse earlier in her life. She advised a psychotropic medication for anxiety and depression.

I was terribly upset by this advice. The situation threw me into an emotional tailspin. I was furious at myself, the dog, the man from whom I had bought her, and the trainer, but mostly, I was furious at my helpless situation. I was not going to give her back, how could I? But could I help her; could I even handle the situation? One day I would be completely in the dumps about what to do; the next day, I would pluck up my determination to make the situation work.

> *von Franz*: a tremendous charge of emotion is generally connected with [the process of the inferior function.] As soon as you get into this realm people easily become emotional . . . you can see the negative side of this connection to the emotions, but there is also a very positive aspect. In the realm of the inferior function there is a great concentration of life, so that as soon as the superior function is worn out—begins to rattle and lose oil like an old car—if people succeed in turning to their inferior function, they will rediscover a new potential of life. Everything in the realm of the inferior function becomes exciting, dramatic, full of positive and negative possibilities. There is tremendous tension and the world is, as it were, rediscovered through the inferior function.[7]

Next stop was doggie day-care—if they would accept her. The trainer suggested that being around other dogs and people would increase her socialization, help her gain self-confidence, and level out her anxiety. With trepidation, I sat in the waiting area for our screening interview. The manager came in, gave me the rundown on procedures and rules, and then said, "I'm going to take B upstairs to see how she does." I was familiar with the term "fear-based aggression." I waited with my own fear to hear if she had attacked someone or crawled under the floorboards from anxiety.

A few minutes later they returned. "She did fine," said the manager casually. "This will be great for her. Bring her next Monday for her first day." I couldn't believe my ears. I was so relieved.

A few weeks went by, and there were no phone calls about bad incidents. Finally, I called to get the report. The manager was enthusiastic: "B is a fabulous dog. Everybody loves B. The dogs love her, the people love her, and she loves everyone. She even has a few special pals she likes to hang around with. There are no problems here."

I was stunned and elated. This was a solid piece of success. However, problems continued at home. By now, I had accumulated a library of dog books about training methods and animal behavior; I studied human–dog bonding, visited websites that described attachment problems of adopting older children, and hired another trainer who was less discouraging. I discovered B was excellent with a Frisbee and loved to chase a tennis ball. I spent hours throwing her the Frisbee—after I learned how (it's not so easy) to throw one. I waited for her to bring it to me and drop it on my lap. Soon she was an expert at flipping it in front of me. Her eye contact with me gradually increased. She would sit and watch me intently until I threw the Frisbee; then run lickety-split, but ever so gracefully, across the lawn; and jump and pull it out of the air, landing like an accomplished ballerina. Later, she would play lap dog, all 40 pounds sitting in my lap while I watched the news. I stroked her ears while she dozed.

> *von Franz*: [The] movement [of extraverted feeling of the introverted thinking type] will be towards outer objects, to other people, but such people will have a symbolic meaning for the person, being carriers of symbols of the unconscious. The symbolic meaning of an unconscious fact appears outside, as the quality of the outer object.[8]

The experience of getting this dog and all that has gone on around her has had the uncanny feel of an enactment, a compelling pull. It has reminded me of the old prophets Jeremiah and Hosea. Those prophets were instructed by God to do strange things without knowing the reasons. Hosea was told to marry a prostitute; Jeremiah was told to buy a new loincloth, bury it in some rocks, then take it out, and wear it after it was spoiled. These enactments were intended to demonstrate, through living experience, the relationship between God and the people of Israel. Jeremiah was enacting the spoiled relationship between God and his chosen people. Hosea was obliged to have the experience of feeling what God felt when the people of Israel went "whoring" around with other gods. Like those old prophets, it felt like "God" had told me to *get a dog*. But *why*?

Edward Edinger: Emerging images from the unconscious may often manifest themselves first in the individual's lived reality. He finds himself—either by his own inner urge and inclination or as a result of some circumstance that comes to him from without—living out a situation that has as its root the symbolic image that he needs to understand.

One place to look for the relevant symbolic images that are emerging from the unconscious is just to look at the way you are living life, what you are doing, and what your inclinations lead you to actually perform. And you may discover that you are doing something like burying loincloths, as Jeremiah did.[9]

The feeling function is that process in us that imparts value to a situation, a person, or an object. This valuation can be positive or negative. Feeling as a function must be distinguished from emotions or actual feelings. For example, just because we are experiencing feelings doesn't mean that we are using our feeling function. Equally, we can have thoughts or ideas without using our thinking function. The feeling function creates a value-toned relationship between me and an "other," but the other also can be myself.

When the feeling function is inferior, the evaluation process can seem autonomous and out of control and the person may feel like an unwitting victim of positive or negative judgments and excessively vulnerable to the feeling judgments of others.

von Franz: The sudden change in his judgment would indicate the inferior feeling. People are very easily influenced when it is a question of their inferior function. Since it is in the unconscious, they can easily be made uncertain of their position.[10]

I describe myself as having inferior feeling, but at my age this function hasn't gone without development. Any life that is fully lived demands a feeling function, and this is especially true for women. To be an effective analyst requires considerable development of the feeling function, inferior or not. Adopting B made me painfully aware of problems and deficiencies in that area of my psychology. I had a living experience of my inferior feeling. I would fall into hyperemotionality, becoming anxious, angry, or despairing. My feelings toward her would swing back and forth. Sometimes I loved her, sometimes I didn't like her, and sometimes I positively hated her. I was vulnerable to the opinions of other people; the last person I spoke with would determine my feeling for her until the next person voiced one. In painful parallel, my relationship with B mirrored an inferior *internal* relationship with myself. When I was in the grips of negative affect about B, I was dogged by negative judgments about myself. "How could you feel that way?!" I would remonstrate myself. I also knew that B could sense my moods and feelings, which would affect her behavior. When I felt hopeful and confident that things would work out, her anxiety-based behavior seemed to diminish. When I was freaked out, so was she. We were quite a pair, all right.

von Franz: The symbol of the dog stands for what we reject and throw away because it seems useless. It is also what we take as being banal and self-evident, the naked facts of life so to speak. Within that dung or "ashes" lies hidden the creative activity of God which constantly sustains our existence. It is through the experience of love that we most frequently discover this hidden miracle of Being. It is the same as what Jung calls in his "Memories" "being connected with the infinite."[11]

We reject all sorts of things that belong to us: feelings, thoughts, intuitions, even the feeling function or the thinking function, or any function if it doesn't work easily, efficiently, if it is slow or too impulsive for comfort. However, to make contact with the "hidden creative activity of God," we need all our functions, especially the inferior function, for that is the doorway to the deeper self.

B became a living symbol of unwanted feelings, the feeling function, as well as unwanted and unrecognized aspects of myself. I felt set up, "hustled" to take on this dog-project that would give me such anguish, but which, I recognized, was providing necessary access to unwanted, rejected parts of my psyche. No wonder, then, was I suspicious of the man with the dog that I went to visit on Thanksgiving Day.

In her book on Arabic alchemy, von Franz commented on a text in which the philosopher's stone is equated to a dog:

the author calls this [stone] a dog and writes a long passage on the exalted mystical qualities of this "dog." . . . [O]ne must remember that the dog is for the Arabs a despised animal and a word of insult. In Sufism and Sufi poetry the dog plays an important role as a symbol of the Nafs, the instinctual psyche. On the one hand it is the vile prima materia on which the novice has to work, on the other hand this "low" unknown factor in man contains the divine secret, the impulse towards individuation. According to Sufi tradition the mystic Bistami had conversations with a dog in which the dog taught Bistami greater humility and greater submission to God. Among other things the dog says: "I have never put a bone aside for tomorrow, but you have a whole barrel of wheat for the future." Bistami exclaims: "I am not even worth being the companion of a dog, how then can I be the companion of the Eternal? Honor to God who educates the best creatures (man) through the lowest one."[12]

This idea of the ego being taught by lower, less developed aspects of the personality is not new in Jungian psychology. In analysis we learn of the wisdom and knowledge that lie hidden in our shadow and instincts. We learn how useful it can be to look at dreams given by the unconscious, our "lower" nature, to find renewal and greater wholeness.

Von Franz continued:

In psychological perspective the dog symbolizes absolute reliable loyalty, completely faithful eros. The real dog has come over from the wild animal to the side of man. He is more domesticated than any other animal. He therefore symbolizes a union of the opposites of animal instinct and cultural consciousness. That is why in our text he mitigates the violence of fire (driven passion) and makes the colours appear, i.e., the nuances of a more differentiated human feeling.[13]

In a recent book, it is claimed that dogs never lie about love. I'm not sure it is love that dogs don't lie about. One trainer told me that dogs must establish a bond to survive; this fact leads them to bond even with cruel owners. (We know that children will do likewise.) Dogs form a bond with humans that is powerful and strong. This bond of attachment has led to stories of miraculous deeds dogs have performed for their human companions, traveling hundreds of miles home, standing watch over a dying or dead human, and all sorts of rescue stories. Whether it is loyalty, in the human sense, or a powerful instinct-based attachment is uncertain. I frequently hear the image of a dog in dreams of people who have a defective mechanism for being loyal to the deeper values of oneself; the dog is a symbol of the instinct for loyalty to oneself or to an "other."

> *New York Times*: Few relationships are so laden with mutual benefit as that between man and dog. Much of the credit for this unusual state of affairs, it now turns out, may lie on the canine side of the equation. . . .
>
> [A study shows] that although chimpanzees may have brain power of far greater wattage, there is one task at which dogs excel, that of picking up cues from human behavior. This interpretive skill was perhaps the ability for which they were selected. . . .
>
> Wolves, though very smart, are much less adept than dogs at following human cues, suggesting that dogs may have been selected for this ability.
>
> Dr. Ray Coppinger, a dog behavior expert at Hampshire College, . . . believes that wolves domesticated themselves. . . . Wolves, which are scavengers as well as hunters, would have hung around the campsite for scraps, and those that learned to be less afraid of people survived and flourished, in his view.
>
> "It was natural selection—the dogs did it, not people," Dr. Coppinger said.
>
> When two species live together for a long time, each usually influences the genetically conferred qualities of the other. People may have selected preferred abilities in the dog, but dogs too may have fostered their favorite qualities in people—not of course deliberately but simply by giving people who used dogs a better chance of surviving than people who did not.
>
> If people and dogs have been living together for a long time, "there would have been some co-evolution of traits that made them function together better," Dr. James Sherpell [expert on dog behavior at the U of Pennsylvania] said.[14]

Recent studies on the evolution of the dog alter previous theories in which dogs were believed to have been tamed and domesticated by early humans. In those theories, humans were active whereas wolves were passive in the process of domestication. Current research suggests the idea that the human–dog relationship has always been mutual, active, and reciprocal.

A reciprocal and mutually beneficial relationship between the ego and what Jung called the Self is the goal of individuation. The Self (spelled with a capital S to differentiate it from more conscious personal aspects) is the transpersonal center of the personality. For Jung, the God-image is the same as the Self. However, the term "God-image" usually refers to those transpersonal aspects of the Self that are shared by a collective group of individuals. A relationship between the ego and this transpersonal center always exists; however, the dynamic interplay between the two comes into awareness with increasing consciousness. In *Answer to Job*, Jung wrote that we are on the verge of an evolutionary leap in the development of the God-image, the collective Self, that is, collective consciousness.

> *Edinger*: [The God-image] is a primary formulation of how mankind orients itself to the basic questions of life, its mysteries.[15]
> On the one hand, the God-image has within it a latent dynamic tendency to evolve and develop. On the other hand, there is evidence to indicate its development and dynamism results from the feedback it receives from conscious egos.[16]

In terms of this reciprocal relationship: the task of the ego is to see "this new God-image, as it lives itself out in one's own individual psychology, as well as the psychology of the collective."[17]

The relationship between a human and a dog closely describes the relationship between ego and Self, especially those aspects of the Self that want to be included in the current transformation of the God-image. We are familiar with the play on words that *dog* and *God* have provided such as "Dog is my co-pilot." From the perspective of the unconscious, and as we heard in the text on Arabic alchemy, the dog and the divine are very close. Instead of holding an image of the Self as a wise divinity figure within, perhaps it is more useful and closer to actual experience to think of the Self as a dog. A dog is much less conscious than a human yet has vastly superior instincts and senses (most notably the sense of smell). But dogs don't think very well. Von Franz wrote an amusing story about her dog, which frequently would come to wrong conclusions. Humans have the potential for a vastly "superior" consciousness, yet the price of this development has been a great separation in the psyche between human culture and animal instinct. When pushed or under extreme circumstances, a domestic dog can become dangerous and revert to its destructive nature by attacking or biting. We, humans, are faced with our own destructive natures made even more dangerous by our advanced technology, whether it is an SUV on the highway or an atomic bomb.

We are currently in a revolution in how we view, collectively, the relationship between humans and animals. The animal rights movement has gained considerable momentum and media coverage in recent years. The discovery that animals possess intelligence, sensibility, and sensitivity clearly disproved the automaton attribution that had dominated our view of animals from the time of Descartes. It is hardly conceivable that people once believed that animals do not experience pain. I wonder if these collective changes are an external manifestation of a rapprochement within the human psyche between animal nature and the rational mind and, therefore, a mirror of a transformation of the "God-image" to include the "dog-image."

Instead of training horses using oppressive tactics to "break them," horse trainer Monty Roberts advocates creating a trusting partnership between horse and human. He describes the process of "starting a horse"; he approaches a horse by communicating through body language. Understanding the basic temperament of the horse, he works with the currents of subtle movement and response between himself and the horse.[18]

Dog training methods, too, are in the process of a revolution that generates heated arguments among trainers. The most progressive and enlightened trainers use only reward-based methods, replacing the older punishment methods. Humans are still taught to embody the role of "alpha," not to intimidate or dominate the dog, but out of respect for the biological needs of survival that are inherent in the social hierarchy of dogs and wolves. It is mutually beneficial for both humans and dogs that humans assume the "top dog" role in the relationship.

This analogy applies to the relationship between the ego and the Self. We need to study the nature of the Self, bearing in mind that it is the source of both wisdom and destructiveness, which are inextricably intertwined and inherent in its nature. The ego can look to the Self for guidance and knowledge, but the ego must question what comes up from the unconscious. The reciprocal feedback relationship that is lived in the human–dog relationship is very similar to what is required of us when we move into the lived, felt experience of the new God-image.

Several years ago, I had a dream in which I was part of a specialized team working to diffuse and dismantle a nuclear bomb. We were working on the innermost mechanism. It was tricky and exacting work, and we were not sure what we were doing. During the discussion of the dream, my Jungian analyst remarked, "You know, the Self is booby-trapped!" Any time we attempt to deal with the deepest levels of the psyche, we are dealing with a dangerous entity. It could blow up in our faces at any time. This notion of the Self doesn't contradict but adds a crucial dimension to the ideas of the Self as an inner guide and source of wisdom. Joining these two perspectives creates the difficult notion of the paradoxical God-image, the Self, which Jung was at pains to describe in his later writings, especially in *Answer to Job*.

Sometimes, in the course of my current dog-project, I have had to manage volatile and potentially explosive emotions that got activated. In addition to my actual dog being a living symbol of the Self, she has been a catalyst (or, perhaps, a *dogalyst*!) for integrating these particular experiences and diffusing dangerous "nuclear" energies.

Entering into a relationship with the Self, the deeper layers of the unconscious, is a tremendous responsibility, full of peril and uncertainty. The ego carries so much responsibility that it can be nearly unbearable. No wonder might we prefer to think of the Self as *only* a source of inner guidance. Such a conception, however, retains the one-sided goodness that is characteristic of the Christian deity, the old God-image, and leaves the job only half done. To participate in the transformation of the God-image, we must, like the prophets of old, enter into a relationship with the Self not knowing how we might be utilized by the powers of the unknown psyche. When it comes to the Self, we cannot say, "No, I'll think about it." There is no returning it to the breeder; nor can we drop it off at the animal shelter or take it to the vet for euthanasia if it becomes too aggressive or otherwise problematic. Usually, by the time we recognize we are in a quandary with the Self, it is too late to do anything but follow through with the project.

von Franz: It is amazing how deeply the inferior function can connect one to the realm of the animal nature within oneself.[19]

I received a Halloween card last year. The picture showed a little boy in his Halloween costume carrying a trick-or-treat bag. He was running down the street yelling "MOM!" pursued by a pack of barking neighborhood dogs. The caption read: "It didn't take Tommy long to regret his choice of Halloween costume." In the picture, Tommy was dressed as a fire hydrant.

This card portrays an amusing predicament between dog nature and a little boy. But on a collective level, it speaks profoundly to the human dilemma today. Are the dogs chasing after Tommy to piss on him? To attack him? To get his candy? Tommy is screaming: "MOM!" wanting rescue by a powerful parental figure.

There is no more Mom, or Dad, or other omniscient, omnipotent figure to rescue us. Instead, as Jung wrote, the tables have turned and now God needs man. That is, the Self, evolving collective consciousness requires individual human consciousness to recognize, humanize, and contain its own powerful instincts. As the Halloween card shows, transpersonal energies are chasing down the human psyche to make a connection and bond. Like Tommy, we are terrified because we do not know what they want or what we can do. And like Tommy, we have truncated arms that are unable to handle the situation, unless or until we grow the capacity to do so. We may need to teach those dogs within, for instance, that survival and being "right" are not necessarily the same. (Remember, dogs don't think well!) Superiority, competitiveness, and rivalry, which are necessary as part of our biological survival heritage, when unleashed upon the world in unmitigated force lead to nuclear wars, religious fanaticism, and exploitation of other peoples. *Inflation* is a relatively tame descriptive that we apply to individuals who are possessed and identified with such states. *Evil* is the descriptive used to refer to a harmful mass or collective phenomenon.

von Franz: The fourth function is always life's great problem: if I don't live it, I am frustrated and half dead and everything is boring; if I live it, it is of such low level . . .[20]

To assimilate a function means to live with that one function in the foreground. . . . Going to it and staying with it, not just taking a quick bath in it, effects a tremendous change in the whole structure of the personality.[21]

It is almost 16 months since I first brought B home. She is a lively, energetic, confident dog—intelligent but a rascal. She's no longer called Mini-B, but either *Bebop*, the name my husband gave her because of the way she "bops" around the house with a toy in her mouth, or simply as Bea, short for Beatrice, Latin for "bringer of joy" and Dante's guide in the *Divine Comedy.*

It is by no means a smooth ride. She still goes crazy when the gardeners invade her territory with those noisy machines. I tell her firmly that they are "friends" and she needs to quiet down. That's one of her jobs that she doesn't much like. My job includes taking her for frequent walks, even when I don't feel like it. I still get upset at times with this dog-project.

Bebop and I have gone through several trainers, each with something useful to offer. We've gone sheep herding and currently do agility training, which has proven an excellent activity for her talents and my limitations. Agility requires a precise working relationship and physical coordination, which is challenging. "By the time you finish this training, you will believe your dog has eyes on the back of her head," said the agility trainer. It's true; a dog's peripheral vision is excellent. If I am not facing or leaning just exactly the right way, I throw her off course. She's always way ahead of me.

There was never anything wrong with her, and I learned recently from the "suspicious" man that she had not been abused in her early months. Instead, her difficult behavior was the product of a lack of experience and exposure to different stimuli. She is a highly sensitive dog. I've now been around many border collies, and she's right in there with them. A current trainer, familiar with her breed, remarked: "Border collies can be quirky—you have to learn what works for your particular dog."

I am aware that I am addressing an external level and a symbolic level at the same time. Each individual Self can be quirky—one must learn what works for this particular Self. My former analyst used to say, "You have to experiment and see what works with the Self. See what you can get away with, and what you can't."

> *von Franz:* If you think of the turning point of life and the problems of aging and of turning within, then this slowing down of the whole life process by bringing in the inferior function is just the thing which is needed. So the slowness should not be treated with impatience and with trying to educate "the damned inferior function"; one should rather accept the fact that in this realm one has to waste time. That is just the value of it, because that gives the unconscious a chance to come in.[22]

I spend a lot of time these days taking walks, practicing jumps, cross-overs, and recalls in my backyard, and going to agility class and the dog park on weekends. Sometimes I feel like I'm wasting time, a lot of time. I get impatient because I'm not writing the books that I think I'm supposed to write, that I'd planned to write, at this stage of my life. Maybe later. Or maybe, in another lifetime, another incarnation, I'll return as someone with extraverted feeling as my primary function. Then when it is time to work on my inferior introverted thinking, well, I'll just have to slow down and waste time writing some books.

Notes

1 Marie-Louise Von Franz and James Hillman, *Jung's Typology* (New York City: Spring Publications, 1971), 54.
2 Von Franz and Hillman, 42.
3 Von Franz and Hillman, 12–13.
4 Von Franz and Hillman, 107.
5 Von Franz and Hillman, 7.
6 Von Franz and Hillman, 42.
7 Von Franz and Hillman, 11.
8 Von Franz and Hillman, 7.
9 Edward F. Edinger, *Ego and Self: The Old Testament Prophets* (Toronto: Inner City Books, 2002), 51.
10 Von Franz and Hillman, *Typology*, 53.
11 Marie-Louise Von Franz, *Muhammad Ibn Umail's Hall Ar-Rumuz (Clearing of Enigmas)* (Switzerland: Verlag, 1999), 168.
12 Von Franz, 163.
13 Von Franz, 165.
14 Nicholas Wade, "From Wolf to Dog, Yes, But When?," *New York Times*, November 22, 2002, National edition, sec. A18.
15 Edward F. Edinger, Dianne D. Cordic, and Charles Yates, *A New God-Image: A Study of Jung's Key Letters Concerning the Evolution of the Western God-Image* (Wilmette, IL: Chiron Publications, 1996), xiii.
16 Edinger, Cordic, and Yates, xix.
17 Edinger, Cordic, and Yates, xxii.
18 Monty Roberts, *The Man Who Listens to Horses* (London: Arrow, 1997).
19 Von Franz and Hillman, *Typology*, 58.
20 Von Franz and Hillman, 62.
21 Von Franz and Hillman, 59.
22 Von Franz and Hillman, 8.

Chapter 3

Violence and the Religious Instinct

I live on a quiet suburban street in Santa Monica, California. Every few weeks, protestors from an animal rights group stand on the sidewalk across from my neighbor's house, chanting, waving placards, and yelling loudly. Soon the street fills with police cars that block traffic. The protestors purport that my neighbor is a vivisectionist conducting research on primates at UCLA. I don't know the veracity of their claim, nor have I ever met the man in question, but the loud noise of the protestors and the cops bring people, including myself, outside. It sends a shiver in me, not because there is anything bad going on, but because the *imminent sense of violence* fills the air. What might happen? The protestors eventually leave, the crowds disperse, and the police cars gradually drive away. Early one morning, this neighbor's car was firebombed, and other researchers living in the area received threatening letters and had rocks thrown through the windows of their homes.

We are fascinated and frightened by violence. How many films, video games, and television shows there are in which violence is prominent and compelling? We are also repulsed by violence. We condemn it, moralize it, and seek ways to reduce or eliminate it. Violence is a ubiquitous reality. It is imperative that we find ways to explore violence, deepen our understanding of violence, to penetrate into the nature of violence.

My lifelong interest in the darker sides of human nature goes back as far as I can remember. Whatever happened during my formative years left me with a curiosity and a need to understand myself and others: what is it that makes us such a violent and destructive species? As a corollary to this question, there is a conversation I have with myself that has been going on for a very long time. It is an inner discussion around the question: "Why can't I just be a nice person?" As a child, I observed adults who acted badly and who were dishonest and destructive. I also observed others who seemed to be genuinely nice people. I aspired to become one of them.

Over the decades I strived to be kind, compassionate, loving, understanding, giving, empathetic, and sympathetic. In many respects, I have become a nice person. But I also know my unkind, not nice, sides, where I can be destructive, self-destructive, and violent. I've destroyed objects and I've ruined relationships. I've been mean and hateful. But I've held tightly to the belief for many years that with

DOI: 10.4324/9781003434009-4

enough soul searching, enough analysis, self-reflection, self-discipline, insight, revelation, transformation, meditation, illumination, active imagination, willful effort, and even prayer, I could become a thoroughly nice person.

Awareness of my dual nature is probably why I was depressed throughout my early life. I became very depressed during my first pregnancy. I thought at the time it was due to the enormous changes that a child would bring, and, of course, in part it was. But later I realized that I was also anxious that despite my best intentions and efforts of will, I would become a mother like my own, cold, uninvolved, critical, and rejecting. There were understandable reasons why my mother was that way, but the experience of catching a strong shadow projection from her made me painfully aware at a young age, at a premature age, that people can have a loving side but also a hurtful, destructive, and even a violent side that shows itself unpredictably.

I experienced my mother as violent even though she never hit me or abused me physically. It was the violence of rejection, hatred, and disconnect. Oh, the reader might think, but is rejection violence? Probably more important is that I experienced my mother's love as violent. My young psyche became a repository for her unbearable emotions. This "trash can" function I provided for her is what clinicians call the process of projective identification. I sensed an onslaught of her outrage, depression, and helplessness. I was conceived during WWII and born while my father was away serving in the army. How could she not have ambivalent feelings about me? How could she not be preoccupied with him, whether he would return, understanding but still outraged that he enlisted and left her alone with two very young children? But while I could feel her disconnect, her distance, and even hatred at the sight of me, I also knew that she loved me. It was a violent love, which sounds oxymoronic, a contradiction. But against our will, our emotions can be powerfully contradictory.

I suspect that my interest and my search to understand the perplexing nature of my mother, myself, and others around me were a deeply compelling reason why eventually, after a detour into a career as a musician, I became a psychologist and Jungian analyst.

When I was in the analytic training program, I came upon Jung's ideas of sacrifice and was especially compelled by the violence in the animal and human sacrifice material because violence seemed a necessary and intrinsic aspect of authentic religious ritual. I had a hunch that there was a vital connection between violence and the religious nature of the psyche. I observed the paradox that strong religious convictions can both prevent and instigate violent behavior.

I read whatever I could lay my hands on about sacrifice in mythology, anthropology, and psychology. Frequently, a creation myth involves the destruction of an original giant or primal man, called the "first victim." This primal being is chopped up to form parts of the world: heaven, earth, mountains, oceans, vegetation, animals, and humans. In anthropology, animal sacrifice was universal as an offering to the gods and remains widespread even today. Human and child sacrifice was more common than we might want to believe. The Aztec ritual of extracting the still-beating heart from a sacrificial victim is a notable example. By observing and collecting dreams, I discovered that the bloody and violent history of human sacrifice, which we think is long in our past, is very alive in the human psyche. I wondered why the psyche speaks in such vivid and bloody imagery.

My interest was compounded by my own dreams particularly one that occurred a few years before I began training:

> I was in a foreign country in some earlier time period. An elaborate ceremonial gown was put on me and I was fussed over in preparation for a big event. Then I was led down and around and eventually up to a platform. It seemed to be a ritual that I was to take part in, and there were priests and attendants along with a large crowd of people. As the dream proceeded, I became increasingly aware that I was to be ritually sacrificed. The dream ended as I was handed a ceremonial knife. I woke up with the shocking realization that I had to perform the sacrifice upon myself.

This dream was disturbing. I did not know how to make sense of the dream, and I had few associations. Most dreams relate in some way to our current life, and, usually, those dreams have many associations. A few dreams cast a shadow forward into the future, and, in these cases, there is a notable lack of associations.

My interest in the imagery of sacrifice culminated when, as a fledgling analyst, I gave a six-week training seminar at the Los Angeles Institute on the Archetype of Sacrifice. I explored how this archetype works and its dynamics and purpose and demonstrated how alive it is today. Although animal sacrifice is an important aspect of that archetype, it was human sacrifice that really interested me, and, in a sense, all my studies were an elaborate amplification of my own dream. In short, animal sacrifice represents a transformation of purely instinctual nature into the culture of an ego complex. Human sacrifice represents a transformation of the ego complex into a relationship of the ego to the larger Self.

I use the term "Self" with a capital "S" to differentiate it from the self that refers to the subjective feeling of the ego. Jung used Self as a way of naming the comprehensive entity that we are or are going to become. The Self includes our consciousness, the ego, but the unconscious as well; it is the larger me, the future, and even one's fate. Jung referred to the Self as "the larger personality."

After his break with Freud, Jung became depressed and, as a result, his unconscious became highly activated. He was forced to engage in his first "active imagination," and around the same time he had the following dream:

> I was in the Alps . . . with another man, a curious shortish man with brown skin. Both of us carried rifles. It was just before dawn, when the stars were disappearing from the sky, and we were climbing up the mountain together. Suddenly I heard Siegfried's horn sound out from above, and I knew it was he we were going to shoot. The next minute he appeared high above us, lit up by a shaft of sunlight from the rising sun. He came down the mountainside in a chariot made

of bones. . . . Presently, around a bend in the trail, he came upon us, and we fired into his breast. Then I was filled with horror and disgust at myself for the cowardice of what we had done. The little man with me went forward, and I know he was going to drive the knife into Siegfried's heart, but that was just a little too much for me, and I turned and fled. I had the idea of getting away as fast as I could to a place where "they" could not find me. As I ran, there broke upon me a perfect deluge of rain, and I awoke with a sense of relief.[1]

Jung was horrified by his dream, but years later, he wrote:

It was a case of destroying the hero ideal of my efficiency. This has to be sacrificed in order that a new adaptation can be made; in short, it is connected with the sacrifice of the superior function in order to get at the libido necessary to activate the inferior function.[2]

Jung realized that he was identified with a heroic attitude of "where there is a will there is a way." Only by sacrificing that attitude, killing it off, could Jung enter and have an experience of the collective unconscious in such a way as to know it from the inside out. Otherwise, his superior function of intellect would never have let him make the descent into the underworld.

The violence of sacrifice is inextricably related to the process of psychological development, individuation, and any significant increase in consciousness. However, I was stumped by the following dilemma: I had carefully discussed and differentiated what I called authentic sacrifice from neurotic sacrifice, but it didn't seem sufficient. I remained perplexed by the conundrum of sacrifice as a genuine act emerging from the religious instinct versus sacrifice as a masochistic or a neurotic act. In masochistic sacrifice, the intention is to propitiate a harsh superego, an internal critic masquerading itself as a threatening god (also called masochistic surrender). In a neurotic sacrifice, the goal is to keep anything from changing. It is a thorny and problematic issue within Jungian psychology to differentiate when one is making a sacrifice that is required for genuine psychological growth from when instead it is a masochistic or otherwise neurotic act that sends one nowhere except around in vicious circles. It is quite difficult to sort out when an act of self-sacrifice is in the service of individuation or when it is an evasion of individuation. The trouble, and why I was stumped, is that these are not easy to differentiate; nor are they always mutually exclusive. Often there is something of both involved in any living example. My dream in which I was required to perform the sacrifice upon myself foreshadowed my struggle to sort out these differences as best as I could. This difference is crucial because only authentic sacrifice has the power to prevent and stop violence.

In mythology, neurotic sacrifice isn't even called sacrifice; it is a tragedy. Consider the story of Medea from Greek mythology. Gifted in the magical arts, she helped Jason obtain the Golden Fleece. Later, Jason left her for another woman and Medea killed the two children she had with Jason. One would never consider what she did as a religious child sacrifice: it was an act of retaliation toward her husband who had betrayed her. The murders didn't serve any purpose but as an enactment of self-serving vengeance.

The Very Nature of Violence Is That It Is Self-Propagating

An act of violence incites another act of violence through retribution, revenge, and reprisal. Sacrificial rituals in anthropology have a powerful, profound purpose: they stop a pattern of vengeance and reprisal. An authentic sacrificial ritual utilizes violence as a method to stop a pattern of vengeance and reprisal that violence sets off. Often a scapegoat is utilized, a sacrificial victim that is agreed upon by the entire group. The victim is usually revered and honored, then loaded with blame and contempt, and then the victim is sacrificed or driven out of the group to die in exile. This ritual dissipates violent, hostile tensions in the group and re-establishes harmony and a feeling of well-being. The "bad thing" is gone, at least for a while. This pattern may be found in the story of Jonah and the Whale, Oedipus Rex, Zorba the Greek, and the story of Christ. An analogous contemporary ritual is our system of capital punishment. The powerful urge to find a scapegoat for violence contributes perhaps to the inability to dismantle this aspect of our judicial system. After an execution, momentarily, justice is served, the victim's outrage mollified, vengeance appeased, and the "bad thing" is gone. Society can breathe more easily—at least for a short while.

In the *New Yorker* magazine, a short story was published that generated more letters and controversy than any story before or since. It is called "The Lottery" by Shirley Jackson.[3] It begins in a small bucolic generic town in the rural USA. It is an annual event that has the feel of a family picnic. All the townsfolk gather; there is great excitement and anticipation. People come together and draw pieces of paper from a box. They hush and hug each other when a blank piece is drawn. Then when someone draws a paper with a black mark on it, the mood abruptly shifts. The gentle townsfolk gather their stones and rocks and begin the annual ritual of stoning one of their members to death.

This story reveals several hard-to-digest realities: under the surface of civilized humans lie murderous, scapegoating, violent tendencies. These are there not because we had bad mothers, but because we are human. The yearly ritual of selecting one of their own at random suggests that any one of us could be the victim of violent scapegoating. I wonder if my neighbor up the street, the so-called vivisectionist, presents as an excuse for people to vent their frustrated hostilities. He is someone that a large group can agree is a bad person. He is a hook for the scapegoat projection. The particularly horrifying aspect of Shirley Jackson's story is that there is no hook; the victim is selected entirely at random.

I am a psychologist, not an anthropologist or sociologist, and my arena for investigation is the individual. Here we find the reverse of mythology: sacrifice generally is the neurotic version. A common example is when there is propitiation to a harsh, fearsome god within what we designate as the archaic critical, murderous superego—murderous because it can attack and undermine one's very will to live. This kind of superego needs constant appeasement to ward off its wrath and attack.

In my clinical work, I hear analysands who describe when they have done something violent, even something relatively minor, they have a spontaneous thought, "I must kill myself." The internal thinking goes: "I am such a contemptuous person, not worthy of any further existence. The world would be better without me." This self-destructive urge can set off a pattern of vengeance and reprisal, what we call an internal cycle of sadomasochism that vitiates the psychological well-being of the individual. This pattern can be difficult to discern from the outside, but it can be felt in the consulting room. One also can sense the hidden inflation: I am so bad; I am the worst person. I deserve death. There is self-reverence along with self-contempt within the neurotic scapegoat victim.

A middle-age single woman brought in the following dream: "I am going to be beheaded. I must put my head in a guillotine. I remember putting my head in. I knew I had to submit to the beheading. Somehow it was all right." The dreamer was afflicted with strong emotional states and a tendency to unleash them in storms of affect that created difficulties for herself and her large family. Her dream indicated that she had to submit to a process in which the original wholeness, the state of being identified with one's affects and emotions, must be dismembered. (Remember from mythology the primal victim that was cut up to create the world!) This woman had to sacrifice her "natural way" of expressing all her feelings. She would say to me, "But I need to be honest and tell them exactly how I feel, don't I?" "Yes," I would say, "in principle, but this doesn't seem to be working; it backfires and keeps you in turmoil and anger at them because they don't change." When they teased and belittled her, she became angry; then they belittled her more, and she continued to be angry. That is a neurotic pattern. I told her, "Yes, someone or something needs to change; but it looks like it isn't going to be them, so it might as well be you."

Violence emerges within the individual when there is a crisis and something fundamental must change. One of two things happens, a real sacrifice or a neurotic one. A titrated dose of violence against violence moves the individual to another level. It is a genuine internal religious ritual that moves the individual to another stage. If a neurotic sacrifice happens, there may be an expression of violence, internal or external, but when the crisis is over, a fundamental change does not occur.

The suicide bomber contains a cluster of archetypal ideas: self-sacrifice, destruction, violence, and catastrophic change. These dynamisms are enacted literally and one-sidedly when the suicide bomber is gripped by a powerful combination of archetypal forces. The suicide bomber is compelled and impelled by the belief that he or she is on a fast track to heaven and union with God. The suicide bomber feels fully supported by family and community to be a sacrificial victim. But it fails to be an authentic sacrifice because it does not accomplish what authentic sacrifice does: it does not quell the violence—that's the hallmark. A suicide bomb attack generates more violence; it propagates violence because it brings about reprisal, usually a violent, repressive response.

In dreams, explosions can indicate the end of a worn-out internal structure. Similarly, catastrophic nuclear explosions and end-of-the-world disasters can indicate the sudden destruction of a world view that creates room for an enlargement of the personality. But not all explosions are positive. Dreams of explosions can also indicate the eruption of affect from a loss of archetypal containment. For example, an abrupt or premature change in the family or therapeutic container can generate a destructive explosion. The suicide bomber is gripped by the need to destroy the status quo to make way for a new world order. He or she feels compelled by the felt will of God to destroy infidels who have turned from God or who worship a false god. This outer situation has an intrapsychic parallel: when there is excessive egocentricity or narcissism, one is worshipping the ego as a false god.

One day I was driving home taking the route I've driven hundreds of times. My mind wandered and I was unaware that a woman driver behind me was impatient with my slow pace. Abruptly she cut around me at a stop sign, made a left turn, and took off. Instantly I gunned my car and took off after her. She ran a stop sign—and so did I. I noticed a bumper sticker on the back of her car which read, "I'd rather be shopping." "I bet you would!" I said as I got right behind her honking my horn. I was gripped with the lust for revenge and justice. I hated her and her fancy black car I imagined was paid for by her rich husband while she spent time . . . shopping! It all happened quickly, but in a moment, I put my foot on the brakes and said to myself, "What the hell are you doing? You are going to get killed and besides, exactly what are you going to do when and if you can catch up with her? Drag her from the car and beat her up? That would make a fine newspaper headline for your colleagues and analysands to read!"

How quickly the urge to retaliate against a perceived injustice is ignited! How the urge grips one into action! The voice that stopped me was stern; it was not a moralistic, blaming voice. I felt my impulse for violence but was able to put the brakes on it. Maybe it is an overstatement, but I sacrificed a natural urge to action and retaliation, an urge that derives from healthy, self-protective instincts.

Violence is a physical or emotional force used to damage, violate, or abuse another. Violence is a word that conveys force, intensity, and transgression. The word "violence" means "treat with force." Violence is a heavily laden word and therefore shocking to encounter when Jung frequently uses it in his descriptions of religious experiences. For instance, if you read his *Answer to Job* closely, you know Jung is writing about his own personal experience and the experience anyone goes through in the course of coming to terms with the unconscious.[4]

In defending the tone of his writing, this is what Jung wrote at the beginning of that book:

> It is far better to admit the affect and submit to its violence than to try to escape it. the violence is meant to penetrate to a man's vitals, and he to succumb to its action. He must be affected by it; otherwise its full effect will not reach him. But he should know, or learn to know, what has affected him, for in this way he transforms the blindness of the violence on the one hand and of the affect on the other into knowledge.[5]

When Jung wrote, *admit to the affect*, he implies that one needs to allow oneself to feel the violence, the outrage, and the desire for action. When an unpleasant and difficult affect arises, resistance in the form of a moralistic response arises at the same time. "I shouldn't feel this way; I should be above such a primitive or childlike affect." It is humbling to admit to an emotion that feels belittling and that one hopes to have outgrown. When Jung wrote, *submit to its violence*, this does not mean becoming identified with violence or being its victim. It means to allow oneself to feel it completely. This is what *penetrates to a man's vitals* means: to allow oneself to deeply be affected by something that is powerful and *other*.

If one is able to engage the affect, then, as Jung wrote, the blindness *of the violence is transformed*. The violence stops propagating, and the impulse for reprisal or vengeance is checked. This is how one can understand the Biblical Job who put his hand on his mouth and said, "I have spoken once, and I will not speak again." This is an example of an internal ritual of self-sacrifice. Jung believed that by his action Job was essentially saying, "Ok, I see what is going on, and the violence, perpetrated by Satan, Yahweh's henchman, stops here."

Jung elaborates on these matters in *Symbols of Transformation* in his long commentary on the epic poem Hiawatha. Here is what Jung wrote about Hiawatha's fight with the primordial corn god, Mondamin:

> [The god] . . appears at first in hostile form, as an assailant with whom the hero has to wrestle. This is in keeping with the violence of all unconscious dynamism. In this manner the god manifests himself and in this form he must be overcome. The struggle has its parallel in Jacob's wrestling with the angel at the ford Jabbok. The onslaught of instinct then becomes an experience of divinity, provided that man does not succumb to it and follow it blindly, but defends his humanity against the animal nature of the divine power. It is a fearful thing to fall into the hands of the living God.[6]

Is the unconscious hostile and violent? Jung implies that violence originates in the non-personal, instinctual layer of the psyche. His statements only make sense from a view that the psyche has both personal and non-personal dimensions. Jungians speak of divine energies and divine affect because it places their origin outside and beyond the purely personal realm of the ego. Violence is an affect that becomes a force or an action. The underlying affect may be anger, hurt, rage, fear, or retaliation; but equally it might be powerlessness, vulnerability, or helplessness, because violence is also a force for self-protection. Jung wrote that we must admit these emotions that assault from within, but one needs to defend one's humanity against being swept up and identified with them. They are numinous and make one feel powerful and omnipotent—like a god. We sacrifice, we give up this feeling like a god, this self-protective mechanism of being God-like, and instead, remain mere mortal, helpless, but with our humanity intact.

Hiawatha wrestles with the corn god for three days until Mondamin finally "yields up his soul and sinks to the ground." Hiawatha buries him in mother Earth and soon "corn sprouts for the nourishment of mankind."[7] This creative harvest results from the intense and violent struggle between Hiawatha and the primal god, the primordial unconscious. This suggests that the struggle with and transformation of violence yields creative energy for wholesome growth and individuation.

In *MDR* Jung alludes to the struggle of the ego with the violence of the unconscious and makes this curious remark: "Jacob wrestled with the angel and came away with a dislocated hip, but by his struggle prevented a murder."[8] Jung doesn't explain what murder is prevented. One understanding is that a premature encounter between Jacob and Esau might have ended in the death of one of them at the hands of the other. Esau might have murdered his twin brother, Jacob, for having stolen his birthright; Jacob might have allowed himself to be murdered out of guilt for his crime; or Jacob might have murdered Esau out of fear of revenge.

Murder is violent repression, rape is a forcible violation, and torture is the sadistic treatment of another. As outer events, they are repugnant, but as archetypal dynamisms, there is another aspect. It seems important to remember that the psyche is not shy about violence, and when necessary, it speaks freely in that language. This is partly as compensation for our misunderstanding of violence. We prefer to believe that most or all violence is bad. Under this mistaken assumption, we can be protective of a destructive neurotic complex that needs to be killed off. We don't want to get involved in any bloody or violent business, even if it promotes psychological health.

Consider the case of a man who was in a relationship with a woman who was more a mother than a lover to him. As a result, his erotic life became dead until he was smitten with another woman. He was in torment and fearful of leaving and losing the first woman. When he did leave that relationship, he had the following dream: "I am on an ocean liner and the murder of a woman, a Glenn Close, a 'fatal attraction type,' was discovered because blood had run onto the deck from behind a closed door. It turned out that at the exact moment that the body was discovered, the ocean liner launched on its voyage." The dreamer was horrified by the image of bloody murder. This meant he had to wrestle with his guilt about what had been necessary for his development. He was tempted to punish himself with excessive guilt, retribution against himself for the violence he felt he had done to the first woman. Eventually, his life became more creative: he married, had children and his work took a quantum leap forward.

Ego consciousness can experience an assault by the unconscious as a rape. This is what Jung referred to in that passage from *CW* 5, *Symbols of Transformation*. Whenever one is assaulted by intense affect, it is what Jung called "the onslaught of instinct." If the intense, explosive affect can be wrestled with and contained, then violence stops. We know that individuation can promote well-being and good physical health. At other times, it takes a toll on one's psyche and body when one must go counter to one's healthy instincts. Remember that although Jacob may have prevented a murder, he *was* injured in the process and left with a dislocated hip.

Chasing down the lady in the black car is the "natural thing" to do, we forget, so much so that we label it pathological, a problem of "impulse control." Normal, civilized life has become a *contra naturam*, against nature. I don't mean to normalize or trivialize violence but to recognize that violence is a crucial, inherent, and necessary aspect of the psyche. Violence is inside us, violence is an inherent shadow side of the religious instinct, and no increment of consciousness happens without a small act of violence.

The tasks of individuation can be experienced as torture. A conflict that can rend and tear one apart is an experience of violence within. Marie-Louise von Franz wrote something remarkable in her little book on *Alchemy*. In describing the experience of suffering a conflict, she wrote:

> If you let yourself be torn in the conflict, then suddenly you change, you change from the deepest root of your being and the whole thing has another aspect. It is as though you tortured an animal so much that it jumped onto a higher level of realization.[9]

What is the attraction to violence in the media? Perhaps it is cathartic to watch violence at a distance and to feel that it is outside and not within. Perhaps it is compensatory for conscious values which strive for peace, love, kindness, and a beneficent god. We want to protect our children from too much violence worrying that it can lead to an increase in violent behavior. There is a pervasive hope that humanity is capable of eliminating violence, and in the infamous words of Rodney King, one day we "might just all get along." This hope is similar to my wish that one day I will become a nice person. I will analyze my complexes so thoroughly that no longer will I be assaulted by intense affect and impulses for violence. I will not worry that a harsh word will slip from my mouth let alone that I will chase after another driver in my car.

We may believe in and strive for love and compassion in our relationships and efforts for psychological growth, but violence appears. Then we often are terribly moralistic, as if violence were a matter easily handled by a personal effort of will. There appears to be gratuitous violence; violence for the sake of violence; glamorizing violence; addiction to violence; and violence that doesn't seem to carry any meaningful symbolic significance. But as Jungian analyst Janet Dallett wrote, "Violence is numinous. . . . Violence occupies the place in today's psyche that sex had early in the *last* century—fascinating but utterly taboo."[10]

Jung wrote:

> The most important of the fundamental instincts, the religious instinct for wholeness, plays the least conspicuous part in contemporary consciousness because, as history shows, it can free itself only with the greatest effort, and with continual backslidings, from contamination with the other two instincts.[11]

The *religious instinct* was Jung's way of formulating what he termed the instinct behind individuation, and the full expression is "the religious instinct for wholeness." Jung agreed with Freud that sexuality is a primary instinctual force and also with Adler that the will to individual significance is a primary instinctual force. These "other two instincts" must be lived fully, as we say, "in the first half of life." The religious instinct is the search for meaning, for something transcending sex and power, ego gratification, pleasure of power, pleasure of sex, something beyond the world of the ego.

If sexuality and will to significance are primary instincts, the religious instinct both serves and counters them and this is the source of *natura contra naturam*, nature against nature without which no significant emotional, intellectual, or spiritual development can take place. The origin of the religious instinct for wholeness is in that layer of the psyche that belongs to all of us and is not predominantly determined by personal historical events. The collective unconscious is the origin of the religious instinct and its shadow aspects, the most prominent of which is violence.

In an interview with Robert Thurman, the Buddhist scholar and father of actress Uma Thurman, in the *New York Times*, Thurman was asked how he felt about the films of Quentin Tarantino in which his daughter has played parts such as *Pulp Fiction* and *Kill Bill*. Thurman replied: "Quentin is kind of obsessed, he's a wild guy. But he is very brilliant. We trust that his motive is to show people the foolishness of violence rather than to glorify it. I hope that's true."[12]

Comedian Bill Maher, in his film *Religulous*,[13] belittles religion as childish and nonsensical. That violence would diminish if people got over their childish need for religion; that we can get rid of violence by realizing how foolish it is; and the overly hopeful idea that collectively humans might become so tolerant of each other, and each other's beliefs, that there is no reason to become violent about anything: these are simplistic ideas that cannot help with the problem of violence.

Violence is built into human relationships from the very beginning. Think of the earliest relationship between a mother and her baby. The baby's crying and desperate neediness violently assault the mother. The needs of the baby, to use the mother's mind and body, place great demands on her. Most mothers would not use the word violent to describe such processes, thinking instead of them as natural, or just being a mother. But in cases where the mother is overwhelmed and not up to the task of containing the violent emotions that assault her, the results are horrifying. What instinctual capacity allows the mother to put up with these assaults? We call it love, or hormonally, it is oxytocin, the love hormone that fosters a deep bond between a mother and her child.

These biological sources of violence become part of the sacred, archetype of the relation between ego and Self, person and God: assault that needs containment, assault for autonomy and significance. Consciousness develops through the process of violent deeds enacted externally and internally. "There is no birth of consciousness without pain,"[14] wrote Jung. But we may equally say that there is no birth of consciousness without violence: violence that is titrated, a homeopathic dosage that is part of a religious attitude.

If one is securely contained within a specific and organized religious context, then there are explanations and methods to manage and contain violence. There is no religious system that does not attempt to bind up the violent tendencies engendered by the human condition.

But what of those who are not contained within a religious context? Jung offers a method of dealing with violence and destructiveness. An inner religious ritual must be constructed. Jung wrote that the individual must "celebrate a last supper with himself and eat his own flesh and drink his own blood; which means that he must recognize and accept the other in himself."[15] In this somewhat grisly act of self-cannibalism, Jung describes a complicated relationship between a person's ego consciousness and the larger personality, the Self. Collisions between the two lead to personality integration. If I had banged into that lady in her big black car, it would have been an enactment of a collision that would have propagated violence rather than ended it.

Basic to depth psychology is to be able to feel our violence, our capacity to be violent without *being* the violence itself, except when necessary. There is a story of a man of sleight build and small stature who startled a burglar rummaging through his house late one night. It was as shocking to the small man as it might have been to the burglar when the small man came after the burglar with a force that caused the burglar to run from the house. We do not infrequently hear of such stories, helpless old ladies beating off attackers with their canes or even their walkers.

Internal conflict is painful and unbearable and at times fills one with intense affect, conflict, and guilt. Violent impulses *can* be generated from the inability to hold these difficult and conflicting emotions. But violence doesn't go away; anything truly new will assault one with force, because a life fully lived moves from one conflict to another. The good news is that the ability to recognize and hold violence increases with experience. It may feel less violent because one recognizes the process.

Jungians speak of violence as a transpersonal force, a power that comes from outside ego will but takes over the ego. Psychoanalysts write about violence as emanating from earliest object relations and primitive mental states. In my clinical experience these are complementary ways of describing the same phenomena. There was a woman analysand who berated me and accused me of incompetence. Her accusations continued for weeks in spite of my earnest suggestions that she find another therapist. She complained that I was failing her miserably; however, she was also attached to me. She demanded that I see her multiple times per week for a minimal fee. During one session, she pressed me with sadistic criticism wondering out loud how I could even call myself an analyst. She continued her attack until I stood up, walked to the door of my office, and said loudly, "Get the hell out of my house." Both of us were astounded at my behavior. She continued to sit on the couch and stare at me. She seemed relieved, said something to that effect, and I sat back down in my chair. While there is more to say about this case, the bottom line is that on the one hand, my outburst indicated that she had "gotten" me; on the other hand, it indicated that she had gotten to me. She was triumphant in unseating me as the analyst, but more importantly, she had been successful, through violent means, in making emotional contact.

Contrast that case with a man who was violent in his politeness, considerateness, and accommodation. He sat in his sessions talking quietly, reasonably, offering only thoughts and feelings that had been well masticated. He wiped out my mind and my ability to think or feel. I was rendered helpless, perplexed, and wordless. I felt sleepy, detached, and ineffectual. Gradually I began to feel angry and full of rage. I got him because he had got to me. Violent communication can be an attempt to make emotional contact.

Blaming and accusations often emerge in the consulting room: blame for the pain of life and for deficits in childhood. An analysand once remarked, "Who asked me if I wanted to be born in the first place?!" These unbearable feelings force themselves upon the analyst, into the analyst, and the natural urge on the part of the analyst is to want to get them out as quickly as possible. The last thing I want is to be blamed or accept the blame for events that happened long before I met the person now sitting with me. But that is precisely what is required of the analyst to stop an internal pattern of violence, vengeance, and reprisal that is sapping the analysand's vital life energy. Not just sympathy or empathy for the child's unmet needs so long ago but present in the room today. The difficult task for the analyst is to offer him or herself to be a willing scapegoat, a sacrificial victim, the person upon whom all the blame can be placed and where it will be accepted without reprisal. The analyst knows that he or she was not the original source of pain, but the process of analysis itself is designed to bring the pain to the surface of awareness, to be felt and to be suffered. Wilfred Bion wrote that a person "who will not suffer his pain fails to 'suffer' pleasure."[16] The analyst says, in effect, I know I am the source of your pain today and you can focus the blame on me. The analyst feels loving and hurtful at the same time and thus suffers the depressive position to pave the way for the analysand to eventually do the same. And in this sacred ritual, something changes, something fundamentally transforms. The violence is held and for a moment the cycle of violence and reprisal, this internal pattern of destruction is halted.

Summary

The nature of violence is that it is self-propagating. One act of violence begets another. Since violence is a shadow aspect of the religious instinct, a ritual of sacrifice can stop the malignancy of violence. A struggle with violence is usually part of the process. A small amount of violence is required, a sort of homeopathic dosage where "like cures like." Finally, the transformation of violence releases creative energy for wholesome growth and individuation.

A sober reflection of violence requires first an attitude *of natura contra naturam*, the ability to hold in check our revulsion, repugnance, and moralistic responses, understandable as they are, toward violence. Only then can one begin to put the brakes on and transform violence. Where do we begin? Not out there where we would like to believe it resides, but in the place where it originates, the human soul. Is this heresy? If so, then all of depth psychology is heresy to the collective standpoint. One postulate of this heresy is that every human being has and should have the capacity for violence.

Finally, if I have cast my net too wide in what I include under the rubric of violence, or if I have narrowed my focus on matters that seem too small, it is with the purpose of capturing something of the essence of violence. Others search in the area of biology, anthropology, or sociology. My area is the soul of the individual, and if we believe what Jung and other depth psychologists have taught us, this is where the work begins.

Notes

1 Carl G. Jung, *Analytical Psychology: Notes of the Seminar Given in 1925*, Bollingen Series 99 (Princeton, NJ: Princeton University Press, 1989), 56.
2 Jung, *Notes of the Seminar*, 48.
3 Shirley Jackson, "The Lottery," *New Yorker*, June 26, 1948.
4 Jung, *Answer to Job*, CW 11.
5 Jung, *Answer to Job*, CW 11, para. 562.
6 Jung, CW 5, para. 524.
7 Jung, CW 5, para. 523.
8 Jung, *MDR*, 344.
9 Marie-Louise von Franz, *Alchemy: An Introduction to the Symbolism and the Psychology*, Studies in Jungian Psychology by Jungian Analysts 5 (Toronto: Inner City Books, 1980), 137.
10 Janet Dallett, *Listening to the Rhino: Violence and Healing in a Scientific Age* (New York: Aequitas Books, 2008), 103.
11 Jung, *Flying Saucers*, CW 10, para. 653.
12 Deborah Solomon, "Seeing the Light: Questions for Robert Thurman," *New York Times*, June 29, 2008.
13 Larry Charles, director. *Religulous*, Lionsgate, 2008.
14 Jung, CW 17, para. 331.
15 Jung, *Marriage as a Psychological Relationship*, CW 14, para. 512.
16 Wilfred Bion, *Attention and Interpretation* (London: Karnac, 1970), 9.

Chapter 4

Fits and Seizures
Dog as Therapist to the Analyst

One morning I was playing Frisbee with my dog, Beatrice, when she suddenly fell over and began convulsing. I ran to her thinking she had ingested a toxic substance in the garden. As her convulsions continued, I believed I was seeing her die right in front of me. I yelled for my husband, but by the time he came outside, Bea had snapped out of her convulsion and was standing looking and waiting for me to throw the Frisbee again. One minute she was in the grips of a dramatic and frightening physical process; the next it was as if that moment had long passed and perhaps didn't really happen at all. Later that day she had a similar episode, and by the next day we were sitting in the veterinarian's office being informed that most likely our dog had "idiopathic canine epilepsy." Idiopathic means that the cause of her seizures is not known and that they are not secondary to another disease process.

Epilepsy is more common in dogs than in any other animal including humans. Primary idiopathic epilepsy is believed to be a genetic neurological disorder in which there is an abnormally lowered threshold for seizure activity caused in part by an imbalance between excitatory and inhibitory neurons.

As a young child, I had terrible temper tantrums. They became emotional fits during adolescence. I could not predict when one would be triggered. I fell asleep on my bed one afternoon after coming home from high school. When I awoke, my skirt had twisted around my body. Instantly in a rage, I ripped it off and then tore it into pieces. I was mortified by what I had done. I had ruined my favorite black skirt, and for weeks I excoriated myself for my uncontrolled destructive behavior. The violence that overtook me was directed at objects, at other people, and toward myself. In my early 20s, I was in a department store waiting to be helped by a clerk who was assisting another customer. There were no other people waiting. By the time the clerk was done with her customer, several other people had come to the counter. I stepped up to be helped, assuming she would know I had been waiting, but the clerk instead told me to take a number. I then noticed others holding numbered slips they had taken from a dispenser. With no intervening thought or feeling, I stuck the woman clerk with my fist and walked out of the store. In an altered state, without feeling anger or rage, I found my car and drove out of the parking lot. I was horrified at my actions and frightened that this could happen so quickly, so "out of the blue."

DOI: 10.4324/9781003434009-5

These fits and emotional storms continued as internal events in adulthood and caused me to feel flawed and humiliated. My fits were mostly out of the notice of others. Whatever was visible was the tip of the iceberg. Inside myself I was perplexed by incomprehensible states that gripped and tormented me. My fits felt like a chaotic jumble of undifferentiated emotions, frequently but not always, a mix of rage and helplessness.

I was upset that I had a dog with a serious flaw. Not just for fun, play, and enjoyment, she would need special attention, medications, visits to the vet, and expensive blood tests to monitor the level of medication. I hated the effects of the medication. At first, it sedated her and made her a bit drunk, even though this abated within a few weeks. I noted the time and duration of her seizures on a calendar. Keeping a careful record allows the veterinarian to precisely adjust the dosage of medication. I wondered if there might be a pattern or relationship between her seizures and events in her environment. Did stressful events make it more likely she would have a seizure? Having a bath? Going to agility class?

We adopted Bea when she was 11 months old.[1] Until she became accustomed to us and integrated into our household, she was overly fearful and skittish. Bea is a border collie: they are smart, focused, agile, and obsessive but also prone to anxiety and fear-based aggression. She was or had all those traits. I did not think to make a connection between her seizures and my internal states until I noticed the following dream:

> I'm on a street and we have our dogs with us. I hear loud noises. It sounds like someone is angry and having a fit and throwing things at a house because he or she got locked out. Then I hear sirens. I walk with Bea down the street and see that there has been an enormous explosion at a place that seems like a school. We are told to stay away because things may be "hot," i.e., radioactive. I see broken dishes that had exploded. I had imagined the noises (from earlier in the dream) came from someone throwing dishes.

The day after this dream, Bea had a seizure and then another seizure the following day. I was startled by the correspondence and wondered if it was just a coincidence.

In my journal, I make notes when I have a fit. Writing out my emotional storms can help me sort out and discover what set me off. I wondered if there was a connection between my own fits and my dog's seizures. I wondered if she was carrying a spillover from me in the psychic field between us. Did she have a seizure from something still deeply unconscious in my own psyche? I observed the similarities between her seizures and my fits: a sudden eruption from deep within the brain/psyche that takes over one's wit and will. I wondered: is a brain seized by a storm that commandeers it into senselessness and uncontrollable jerking like a psyche seized by the spasms of fear, rage, panic, or terror?

Bea stands in front of me or sleeps peacefully when suddenly her body goes rigid for several seconds. This tonic phase is followed by the clonic phase where she thrashes and her body moves rhythmically, her mouth frothing and her jaws clenched. It lasts for no more than one to two minutes, but it seems to go on and on. Then her body stops jerking, and she is momentarily still, deeply unconscious with heavy, labored breathing. After a few minutes of stillness, suddenly she puts her head up as if startled awake from a deep sleep. Disoriented and uncoordinated, she staggers around the house banging into walls and furniture as I attempt to restrain her. Gradually she regains coordination and begins a "trot-trot" of anxious pacing around the house. This post-ictal phase can last for several minutes to several hours.

From inside me, it is equally instantaneous: I am gripped by an intense jumble of emotions. I feel taken over by a force that is larger than my will. I often want to throw something. I once tore a phone off the wall. It can last for minutes, hours, or days. I stumble around inside myself trying to regain emotional footing and a sense of internal stability. In my post-ictal phase, I feel humiliated and ashamed.

Beatrice does not feel ashamed following one of her seizures, only quite thirsty and hungry. Jung wrote,

> for in certain respects the animal is superior to man. It has not yet blundered into consciousness nor pitted a self-willed ego against the power from which it lives, on the contrary, it fulfills the will that actuates it in a well-nigh perfect manner. Were it conscious it would be morally better than man.[2]

What hubris to think that I should or could have control over all vast forces within the psyche? But, of course, I think I should.

I thought long and hard about that dream of the explosion: someone having a fit, being locked out, throwing things in anger. The dream occurred during a holiday break in my analysis at a stage when I was still unaware and unconvinced of the effect my psychoanalyst's absence had on the younger parts of my psyche. Because of that dream, I was able to think about and connect to feelings of being shut out, enraged, and having the urge to throw things. There are dishes in my analyst's waiting room. I could imagine and I could feel myself throwing those dishes at the closed door of his consulting room.

This is a remembrance of how shut out of my mother's mind I had been as a young child. As an infant, I had been unable to get inside her mind/body to access her maternal reverie. As an older child, I made violent attempts to penetrate her, to gain love and attention. These attempts backfired and brought instead rejection and shame. Unbearable feelings that are unable to be contained and metabolized create emotional storms. In epilepsy, the excitation and firing of neurons cannot be stopped. My condition felt likewise: the cells of my emotional mind were prone to unstoppable rapid firing.

While sitting folding laundry, Bea was in her bed next to me. She looked odd. I jumped to her side and realized that for the first time I was observing her in a pre-ictal phase. I held her head remembering that I had read someplace that it is possible to avert a full-blown seizure if one catches it early. But what did one do? I couldn't remember. I held her and called her name and tried to get her to look at me. In this desperate state, I wanted to have an effect on her impending takeover; I made noises, said her name, and sang songs. It seemed like several minutes I carried on in this manner until I finally felt her body go rigid into the tonic phase and then begin the rhythmic thrashing of the clonic phase.

The next day I received a phone call concerning a matter at the Jung Institute that I believed to have been settled. Apparently, my careful planning was about to be undone by a tide of unpredictable events. I became anxious and upset and could feel my body become rigid. An intermixed feeling of helplessness and rage flooded my body and mind. "Be calm," I told myself. "Don't get all worked up before you know for sure what is really going on." My mind and body were racing ahead ready for fight or flight. I noticed the attempt to hold myself, talk to myself, and perhaps avert a full-blown fit. I quickly thought through the possibilities and contingencies: if this, then that, or if that, then I could do this. No, I'd better not do that until I find out about this. Gradually I found a plan of action that seemed to satisfy my sense of urgency and my need to play the situation diplomatically. I felt myself settle down. I made phone calls and relayed relevant information. I received a return call stating the schedule would be kept as previously planned.

I linked Bea's seizure the day before to my fit the day after. Her seizure preceding so closely gave me a warning of my own impending fit. I recognized the similarity between my attempt to interrupt the seizure process of my dog and the attempt to stop my process of going into a full-blown fit. It seemed to bring a strange new meaning to the idea of a "seizure alert" dog.

Some dogs are trained to be "seizure response" dogs. They learn to come to the aid of their human companion once a seizure has begun. Dogs that can "sense" a seizure before it happens, by minutes or even hours, are called "seizure alert" dogs. They are able to alert a person of an impending seizure and help the person get to a safe place before it begins. It is not known how this happens, but dogs can learn it only by themselves; they cannot be taught to anticipate a seizure. About 10 percent of dogs trained to be seizure response dogs over time become seizure alert dogs. In a particularly odd case, reported in the *Los Angeles Times*, in November 2005, a man living in Oregon adopted a dog that became a seizure alert dog when the man subsequently developed seizures secondary to multiple sclerosis. In a strange twist, after the man stopped having seizures, the dog developed seizures with no discernable cause. The man's mother speculated that the dog had gone one step further: the dog learned to have seizures for its owner.

Why, I've asked myself, does one issue trigger an emotional fit while most issues do not, or are easily contained? There seem to be a set of conditions that lower my own threshold for having a fit: I feel forgotten, out of mind, deleted, disregarded, discarded, as if I don't exist. These states precipitate feeling as if I am falling into an abyss, a black hole, or flying off into outer space. The ensuing terror and desperation make me go "out of my mind," and something comes in to take possession of me, something ancient, archaic, and primitive. A screaming, raging fit of emotion saves me from disintegration—a last resort measure but, nevertheless, life-preserving. This process happens instantaneously, or nearly so, and when I watch my dog go through her seizure process, it is as if I were observing myself from the outside in, myself in a dog's body. Hers is an electrical storm; mine is an emotional storm: in both the effects are ravaging.

I first used the term "black hole" to describe to my longtime Jungian analyst states of extreme depression that I fell into. Once I told him about a horrific weekend when I was immobilized by a state of desolation and despair. He asked why I hadn't called him. I described my mental state as being one from which no light escapes. I said, "I was unable to reach out just like nothing can escape the inward gravitational field in a black hole." He seemed to grasp what I described. Many years later, I came across the term in psychoanalytic literature describing certain primitive mental states.

Frances Tustin wrote about her child patients who used the term "black hole" to describe some of their internal psychic experiences.[3] Tustin also wrote about children for whom psychological birth has been a psychological catastrophe. When the mother cannot bear an intense emotional state "and process it by empathy and understanding, the infant experiences a precocious sense of 'two-ness' which seems fraught with disaster. . . . Such children are aware of too much, too soon, too harshly, too suddenly for them."[4] Earliest integrations between sensory experiences of soft and hard, comfort and discomfort, taking in versus pushing out have not taken place. Some children become fused with "hardness," and frustration "is experienced as a tangible irritant, as a hard and painful friction—as roughness. Irritating friction produces rage and panic. When this reaches a crescendo of intensity it results in a tantrum-a fit of temper as we often term it."[5]

Reading the work of Frances Tustin loosened shame and a moralistic attitude I had toward my fits. I was able to feel empathy for myself as a child who experienced attachment disruptions and deficits in infancy and childhood. I also began to appreciate, as Tustin described, that my tantrums had served as a protection against the danger of a disintegrative process with more dire consequences.

James Grotstein wrote in a series of articles entitled "Meaninglessness, Nothingness, Chaos and the 'Black Hole,'"

> The patients' usage of the term [black hole] seems to convey a sense of a catastrophic discontinuity of self, of falling over the abyss into the void. It frequently designates a phantasy of their inner mental geography, connoting a picture of a disrupted landscape with a sudden, unexpected confrontation with a cliff, abyss, or hole which seems to be pulling one over its edge. . . . The "black hole" conveys the experience of meaninglessness and nothingness, and represents the ultimate traumatic state of disorganization, terror, chaos, randomness, and entropy. It is therefore connected to the active and passive phantasmagoria associated with the death instinct and may be its most apocalyptic manifestation.[6]

That someone could write in a way that so accurately described the mental states I experienced was astonishing to me, as was his attunement and empathy.

I found resonance, as well, in the works of Sandor Ferenczi. In a paper titled "The Unwelcome Child and His Death Instinct," Ferenczi wrote, the symptoms of epilepsy express the frenzy of a tendency to self-destruction that is almost free from the inhibitions of the wish to live. . . . I know of cases in which an epileptic attack followed upon painful experiences which made the patient feel that life was hardly any longer worth living.[7]

These words touched on painful suspicions, which my mother always denied, that I was an unwelcome second girl born during WWII while my father was overseas. He was there for my birth, made fun of my appearance, and then did not see me again until I was nearly three years old. I felt an odd pain about myself as a child as if I were somehow a mistake and unwanted.

In another paper titled "On Epileptic Fits" Ferenczi described an epileptic seizure as a profound regression back to the intra-uterine state. It is the unfettered death instinct that pulls the epileptic into a regression, toward being unborn, toward death, as evidenced by the fact that some epileptics actually suffocate during a seizure.[8]

This material spoke profoundly to my life experience and the resulting strength of the "death instinct" in me and its pull to self-destruction. To enter my "black holes" of depression is to enter the viscous experience of miasma where to live, to feel, and to experience is too painful to bear, where all the defenses are gone. There is no energy for anger, rage, or self-righteousness to help me, to bolster my will to live. I want to sink into oblivion. I want to die, to be rid of my sentient self which has become a torment and my enemy. There is something in me that wants to live, but this "life force" is felt only dimly through a density that resists with heavy inertia.

Prior to discovering this material, I feared my fits might be "just" narcissistic rage, borderline emotional volatility, or as people would remark to me, "You just react like that when you don't get your way." I, of course, accused myself of the same thing. While another part felt something else might be going on that I could not understand, my moralistic, superego animus would shut down further thinking. This pattern went on for years.

I focused on discovering if I could help Bea and perhaps reduce her dependence on anti-seizure medications. I took her to my body worker experienced in cranio-sacral techniques. Bea was an excellent patient. She lay on the floor while he felt her cranial bones. She dropped into deep stillness, which is supposed to activate the body's self-healing activity.

After two treatments, Bea was free of seizures for over four months. Although she has a pattern of having fewer seizures in the summer, I was hopeful that I had stumbled upon an auxiliary non-drug treatment. However, in September of that year, she had three seizures and by mid-October, three more. I increased the dosages of her medication. November brought three more seizures and in December there were four. At this point Bea was taking a combination of phenobarbital and potassium bromide.

Dogs are unable to take most of the newer anti-seizure medications for humans because of toxicity or because they are metabolized too rapidly. For 2 and 1/2 years Bea was treated with phenobarbital alone. It is the first-line treatment for canine epilepsy as it quickly and easily controls seizure activity with minimal sedation. It works by increasing the activity of inhibitory neurons. However, phenobarbital can cause liver disease with long-term use or in high doses. When the maximum dosage is attained and seizures are no longer controlled, a second medication is added. The most common one for this purpose is a very old medication, potassium bromide. It is a salt that was used to treat seizures in the past century. It is not commercially available in the USA, so a solution is dispensed by veterinarians or compounding pharmacies. The action upon seizure activity is different from phenobarbital. It works by stabilizing the chloride channels in neuron cells by replacing them with bromide. This in effect increases the seizure threshold.

If you think I understand any of this, I don't. But like a fascination the alchemists had with the chemical components and their actions, my imagination is taken by them as metaphors to apply to myself. How might I increase the activity of inhibitory neurons in myself? How can I stabilize the chloride channels in my emotional brain? Certainly, the analytic work I have done to understand and process my fits has contributed to an increase in my ability to remain calm in the face of triggering events and has brought increased stability within. But no cure, not the cure I had hoped for, and not the cure for my inner demons and torment I had expected, really, all along. I had increased self-control, to be sure, but not a cure.

Jung wrote about psychic forces that confront the ego with overwhelming force. He described his own experience of God: "This is the name by which I designate all things which cross my willful path violently and recklessly."[9] Jung also wrote, "God, as an autonomous complex, is a *subject* confronting me"[10] and "God is an ailment man has to cure."[11]

In addition to personal, developmental explanations for my lifelong fits, are there other factors for my being confronted by this "autonomous complex"? When I move into my "black holes" through my developmental issues, I come to a field that is psychosomatic or somatopsychic, a pre-personal, non-personal, archetypal field. Rather than being ashamed of my unresolved issues with affect regulation, might I think of myself as an explorer of psychic inner space? If I am able to suspend my moralistic self-judgment and look at my experience objectively, from a prospective view, where are my fits leading me?

Many years ago, I had a dream in which I was part of a specialized team working to diffuse and dismantle a nuclear bomb. We were working on the innermost mechanism. It was tricky and exacting work, and we were not sure what we were doing. It was dangerous because, in the process of trying to defuse the bomb, it might explode. During a discussion of this dream with my Jungian analyst, he remarked, "Yes, you see, the Self is booby trapped!" I was startled that he would equate my explosive, destructive complex with the Self.

Exploration of my deepest core complexes has been dangerous and at times seems to unleash more of the very problem I am trying to resolve. I come to the disturbing conclusion that for me God may be an "autonomous complex," but this God has forced itself to be a lifelong work. Not the helpful and benevolent manifestations of the Self, although I am grateful for those; no, my work is with the destructive components of the collective unconscious as they manifest in my psyche.

My "black holes" become wormholes to God, to the Self. Through them, I move into early, hidden, traumatic, personal issues. I emerge into a region that belongs not just to me but to the human condition. The archetypal psyche is experienced as a painful paradoxical reality.

I wanted my dog, Beatrice, to be back to her normal border collie self, a bit too skittish, caring more about playing ball or catching a Frisbee than about her dinner. Border collies work and play for the intrinsic pleasure in the activity rather than for reward. I wanted my hyperactive dog back to normal. I wanted myself back to normal, too, or something people call normal. I wanted not to be so reactive to noises. I wanted not to feel as if my life were walking around a precipice where at any moment I might fall in or something might reach out and seize me. I wanted to cure myself. I wanted to cure my dog. I hoped to cure my dog. I hoped to find a link between us so that if I could go deeply into myself and find the place where she and I are the same, I could bring healing to us both. Is this an arrogant desire? An inflated wish? Magical thinking?

What effect the mind can have on the body, the body on the mind, and how the field between them works is a compelling curiosity. I wonder how my dog is part of this field and what part she plays. I ask, how did I end up with a dog with epilepsy? How did I end up with a dog similar to me in so many ways? High-strung, skittish, and freaked out by loud noises, we are both prone to paranoia or aggression when confronted by something we don't know, understand, or are unable to tolerate.

On Christmas day, Bea had her 20th seizure of 2006. Compared to six in 2005, six in 2004, and four in 2003, the year she was diagnosed, I was discouraged and feared that her epilepsy was slipping out of control. Blood tests revealed she was at maximum dosage for both current medications. Adding any more of either might bring better seizure control but would sacrifice her quality of life and cause a toxic reaction. A new anti-seizure drug was suggested by our veterinary neurologist. "I've had excellent success with this medication with some of my patients. Two beagles (another breed known for epilepsy) were maxed out on phenobarbital and potassium bromide. They started taking Keppra and for one dog, that's all he takes. They have very few seizures and the side effects are minimal. There are two downsides: it is expensive, and it needs to be administered three times per day," she told us. I read about this new drug on websites devoted to canine epilepsy. We added this medication two days after Christmas.

Bea had no seizures for almost six months, so I began to reduce her dosage of potassium bromide until she experienced a breakthrough seizure. Since then, she has remained stable on her three medications experiencing an occasional breakthrough seizure, which is mild, of short duration, and sometimes with no loss of consciousness. She recovers quickly and has no noticeable post-ictal state. There is talk in the field of neurology that over time, and with prolonged use, this new medication, Keppra, may re-stabilize and repair cells that have been damaged during repeated seizures, called the "kindling" process. This parallels the latest work in human neuroscience in which a prolonged and deeply affective psychoanalytic process is thought to facilitate new neural pathways in the brain.

There are notable changes in the pattern of my fits. There is an increased ability to prevent them from taking over my psychophysical system even after one is triggered. I have an embodied understanding that I do not need to resort to becoming God-like, allowing an inrush of omnipotence to over-excite my system and crash through the gates of my chloride channels. I can sense I will be all right in the face of what feels like a catastrophe. I can know God-like states without becoming lost in them, and the need to become possessed by a self-protective omnipotence as an automatic response to threats has greatly lessened. My fits now feel like a coming together of parts of my personality long kept estranged. Over time these events have become less violent and less explosive, as the material is increasingly available for creative integration rather than for repeated self-destructive episodes: nuclear fusion replacing nuclear fission.

Late in August of 2007, Beatrice became ill with what appeared to be simple gastritis. She did not improve after several days of a bland diet. She vomited everything ingested. Tests, X-rays, barium studies, and even ultrasound were inconclusive about her condition, which by now was steadily deteriorating. The vets, veterinary surgeons, and radiologists argued about the possibilities: cancerous growth, pancreatitis, or foreign objects. I felt helpless and frustrated, and I worried about the worst. I was annoyed by the inconvenience and expense her illness was creating. I expressed something to that effect out loud to my husband to which he replied, "You love that little dog." I said, "I don't know if I love her—maybe I'm just attached to her." "Well," he said, "whatever you call it, you are," at which point I became overwhelmed and distraught at the possibility of losing my quirky dog.

We agreed to exploratory surgery, and later when the surgeon called, he described what he pulled out through an incision in her stomach. A rough piece of plastic with a lot of string-like stuff wrapped around it had been lodged between her stomach and small intestine causing a partial blockage and making it difficult to see on the X-rays. Everything else was normal, and amazingly, throughout all the weeks of vomiting, surgery, anesthesia, and recovery, she did not have a single epileptic seizure.

After the crisis settled, I wondered what this might be about given that it occurred as I was preparing to present this paper at an upcoming conference. I remembered that during my earliest preoccupation with Bea's epilepsy, I carried a dark worry that somehow, I had caused her epilepsy. This thought connected to an old worry that I had contributed to the death of my father when I was age 6. The sense of my own destructiveness and these dark, unthinkable, thoughts created an emotional blockage in me. They eventually produced symptoms of the very same nature, that is, my destructive emotional fits.

Feeling responsible for Bea's epilepsy has many strings wrapped around it: negative grandiosity, self-punishment, and a desperate need for a sense of control. Even if I can't correct something back in time, I prefer to hold an illusion in my mind that I can. That complex of foreign bodies, of Beta-elements, finally needed to go: an analytic surgical excision of all that stuff, all the self-loathing, self-blame, and sadomasochistic pleasure I get from thinking of myself as a terrible, bad, destructive person.

Bea's epilepsy and intestinal blockage have served as a mirror and metaphor for my own psychic processes. But is that all? Dogs are particularly vulnerable to psychic infection. There is unconscious communication and communion between dog and human, projective identification, and *participation mystique*. We can make our dogs sick and neurotic and even drive them crazy. But we also can make them well.

How her conditions and mine are interrelated, I can never know for sure. Indeed, she has her own life and fate separate from mine. But I incline toward the view that there is more psychic interaction than not. My dog as "therapist to the analyst"[12] takes on what is deeply unconscious in me. She holds and contains and makes it visible to me. Through a kind of "active imagination," I undergo a re-integrative process that brings about a healing process for dog and human.

Postscript

Beatrice lived a happy dog life for several more years and died of natural causes at age 15, the average life span for a border collie.

Notes

1   See Chapter 2, this book.
2   Jung, CW 9i, para. 420.
3   Frances Tustin, *Autistic Barriers in Neurotic Patients* (New Haven, CT: Yale University Press, 1987).
4   Frances Tustin, "Psychological Birth and Psychological Catastrophe," in *Do I Dare Disturb the Universe? Memorial to W. R. Bion*. J. Grotstein (Ed.) (London: Caesura Press, 1981), 192.
5   Tustin, *Psychological Birth*, 191–2.
6   James Grotstein, "Meaninglessness, Nothingness, Chaos and the 'Black Hole' II," *Contemporary Psychoanalysis* 26 (3) (1990): 377–8.
7   Sandor Ferenczi, "The Unwelcome Child and His Death Instinct," in *Final Contributions to the Problems and Methods of Psychoanalysis*. M. Balint (Ed.), E. Mosbacher (Trans.) (London: Routledge, 1994), 102–3.
8   Sandor Ferenczi, "On Epileptic Fits," in *Final Contributions*, 197–204.
9   Carl G. Jung, Gerhard Adler, and Richard Francis Carrington Hull, *Letters: In Two Volumes*, Bollingen Series, 95: 1–2 (Princeton, NJ: Princeton University Press, 1973), 525.
10   Jung, *Letters*, 571.
11   Jung, *Letters*, 33.
12   Harold Searles, "The Patient as Therapist to His Analyst," in *Tactics and Technique in Psychoanalytic Therapy, Vol II: Countertransference*. Peter Giovacchini (Ed.) (New York: Jason Aronson, 1975).

Chapter 5

Negative *Coniunctio*

Envy and Sadomasochism in Analysis

Introduction

In his non-fiction book *What I Talk About When I Talk About Running*, the Japanese novelist Haruki Murakami wrote the following comments about the process of writing a novel.

> Basically I agree with the view that writing novels is an unhealthy type of work. When we set off to write a novel, when we use writing to create a story, like it or not a kind of toxin that lies deep in all humanity rises to the surface. All writers have to come face-to-face with this toxin and, aware of the danger involved, discover a way to deal with it, because otherwise no creative activity in the real sense can take place.[1]

I would question whether the practice of psychoanalysis is an "unhealthy type of work" but would agree that it can be a dangerous kind of work. When we begin psychoanalysis, we invite a "kind of toxin" to rise to the surface. Whether one calls it shadow, trauma, resistance, destructiveness, envy, or narcissism, when we invite the forces for psychological growth, integration, and individuation to manifest, we also invite the forces of anti-growth, anti-individuation, and anti-life. They are inextricably mixed, not just in pathology, but also in life; the only question is what ultimately gets the upper hand. This question, in one form or another, has preoccupied the field of depth analysis since its beginning.

Jung warned of a latent psychosis as the major risk of undertaking a depth analysis. Freud wrote that for people who are narcissistic or psychotic, psychoanalysis is not possible since the transference that is necessary for treatment does not occur. In the past several decades, psychoanalysts of all schools have sought to extend the effectiveness of analysis to borderline, narcissistic, and psychotic disorders. In the course of this exploration, problematic patterns have surfaced, even in psychoanalyses of neurotic and normal individuals.

Jung wrote, "The *coniunctio* is an a priori image that occupies a prominent place in the history of man's mental development."[2] The *coniunctio* image is derived from alchemy, Christianity, and pagan sources. It is used in analytical psychology

DOI: 10.4324/9781003434009-6

to describe a process whereby two unlike substances are joined together; a related term is the *complexio oppositorum*, where many opposites are embodied in a single image. The *coniunctio* is the birth of something new; it is positive in the sense of growth, development, or individuation.

The central image of the *coniunctio* is a sacred marriage or sexual intercourse between two human figures. In the strictest sense, the *coniunctio* indicates the joining of two aspects *within* the unconscious. However, *coniunctio* is commonly used in other ways including the psychological process between conscious and unconscious, between analyst and analysand, between the conscious standpoint of the analyst and unconscious of the analysand, and the converse.

The *coniunctio* as a constellated archetype between two people becomes a highly charged energy field. This is where danger, as well as new possibilities, arises. When the *coniunctio* becomes enacted between the analyst and the analysand, technically it is "acting out." However, there are situations where this enactment, along with the danger it brings, is a *necessary* stage for any significant psychological development. Any *negative coniunctio* that becomes constellated between the analyst and the analysand is already occurring *within* the psyche of the analysand and to some extent within the analyst. When it becomes a dominant theme in the analysis *between* the analyst and the analysand, this indicates that analysis has become a necessary agent to modify the destructiveness and resistance that it indicates. This is no easy matter.

There are several forms of enactment that I designate as the "negative *coniunctio*"; among them are "envious pairing" and sadomasochism. They are negative because the *coniunctio* does not produce positive development and because it is a defense against growth and change. The negative *coniunctio* might as well be called anti-*coniunctio*; however, if the analysis can undergo a transformation, then negative can change to positive. The key to this shift is not altogether straightforward or easily understood. Diligent consciousness on the part of the analyst, as well as nearly surgical skill and intervention, is essential. In alchemical terms, incubation, "marination," and distillation, as autonomous activities of the psyche, also play a part. Certainly, there is no "waiting around for the psyche to naturally unfold," no "making the unconscious conscious." Helpful here also are the words of Donald Meltzer who described some cases where the analysis is "a rescue operation and cannot be undertaken in safety."[3]

The term *coniunctio* applies to these difficult cases because the powerful archetypal field that is constellated may have a numinous quality. The analyst and the analysand get drawn into a primitive mystical connection (identity) with each other, something that Jung (drawing from the anthropologist Levy-Bruhl) called *participation mystique*. It is a state in which the subject cannot distinguish himself from the object. This is to be differentiated from projective identification, a more active defensive and communicative process, although there may be an overlap between the two. The *participation mystique* that occurs in these cases, a mystical identity, is due to the activation of vital, primitive aspects of the psyche. The identity appears as an *a priori* condition, an initial identification that must undergo differentiation—as if for the first time.

Background

Freudian psychoanalysts, more than Jungians, have written explicitly about clinical material that falls into the category of the *negative coniunctio*. Foremost is Freud's notion of the "death instinct" that he postulated in 1920[4] to explain particular psychological conditions of self-destructive behavior such as repetition compulsion and masochism. These conditions could not be explained solely based on the "pleasure principle." Freud thought that the death instinct was silent and not directly observable. The life and death instincts, according to Freud, play an important role *with* each other. The life instinct has the task of diverting and taming the death instinct. In Freud's view, the "instinct for mastery" derives from a properly modulated death instinct.

The negative therapeutic reaction was described first by Freud in 1923.[5] The negative therapeutic reaction refers to situations where patients react badly to genuinely good interpretations or who get worse rather than better in analysis. This idea was further developed by Joan Riviere (as resulting from guilt), Melanie Klein, Herbert Rosenfeld, and others (resulting from envy). The underlying causes of such failures are attributed one way or another by those writers to derivatives of the "death instinct."

Melanie Klein made use of the death instinct in the development of her work as it provided a theoretical basis for the sadism she observed in the play of children. She felt that many derivatives of the death instinct were readily observable in the clinical setting. Despite this line of development, the "death instinct" did not gain acceptance and still hasn't to this day with much of psychoanalysis (particularly in the USA).

There is an overlap between the negative therapeutic reaction and the negative *coniunctio*; they are both defenses against analysis. The major difference is that in the latter, the analyst gets drawn into a constellated archetypal pattern and becomes an active player in the dynamic. In a negative therapeutic reaction, the analyst may play a lesser role.

Wilfred Bion described different types of relationships that can occur in analysis: symbiotic, commensal, and parasitic.[6] In symbiotic and commensal relationships both parties are beneficial to each other. In a parasitic relationship, destructiveness, in some form, gets the upper hand. This causes the analysis to bog down and become pernicious to both the analyst and the analysand. This is the negative *coniunctio*.

Jung was aware of the dangers of latent psychosis when undertaking an analysis. This was a major reason why, early on, Jung opposed lay (non-medical) analysts. In his later years, Jung seemed less interested in the actual treatment of psychosis and other severe disorders because his attention was taken up with issues of individuation in normal and neurotic individuals.

Jungians write about the "lesser *coniunctio*" in which one opposite absorbs the other.[7] Any analysis, of course, may go through many "lesser *coniunctios*," for example, when the unconscious temporarily overwhelms the ego. But there are many virulent examples that are played out within the analysis between the analyst and the analysand. One not uncommon scenario is when the analysis becomes a process of indoctrination. In this situation, a rigid identification with a particular technique or ideology replaces, obscures, or even obliterates analytic uncertainty, vulnerability, and openness. This lesser *coniunctio* is also a negative *coniunctio* in as much as it is a destructive attack upon and defense against the work of analysis.

These patterns can be highly resilient and resistant to change or modification, let alone transformation. The ego colludes with and protects the dynamic from change so much so that any analysis or attempt to bring it to consciousness is felt to be highly threatening. In the clinical examples described later, the negative *coniunctio* locks two people or two aspects of the personality together in a deadly, destructive, no-win situation, the undoing of which requires painstaking patience and difficult analytic work.

It appears that we need to continually develop more differentiated language and imagery for these processes and we must also be able to contemplate the bizarre and disturbing. If one moves away too quickly to the positive, to resolution, to "wholeness," one can foreclose on what may be gained in the miseries and mysteries of destructiveness and despair.

Envious Pairing

When envy is strongly constellated between two individuals, it creates a negative *coniunctio*. Being familiar with one's own "envy complex" is essential for the analyst and can provide some degree of inoculation. However, in Jungian terminology, envy is archetypal, an inborn pattern. Melanie Klein describes how envy and the defenses against envy are difficult to distinguish. Envy is a primitive mechanism (archetypal) that can never be "analyzed away." In some way, one always remains vulnerable to envy. Analysis is a "set-up" for the emergence of envy. If the analyst does her job well, if she provides helpful understanding and insight, then this can provoke envy in the analysand in the form of wanting to spoil the good helpfulness. "How is it that this person can be so helpful, and how is it that I am so needy and dependent upon this person?" is a common internal lament of the envious analysand. Without awareness that envy is constellated, reactions motivated by shame may be misunderstood or misinterpreted. Paradoxically, if these are understood and handled with compassion and care, envious attacks are renewed.

Case Material

Powerful and painful feelings of envy require considerable ego strength to endure; therefore, envy and its defenses may not be available until later in an analysis. This was the case with the analysand who presented the following dream:

> The tiles in the house were deteriorating: rats and old sick looking cats were coming up out of the floor. I knew I had waited too long to sell my house. Even

if we repaired all the tiles, the inspectors would pick up on it. They wanted me to take some of the sickly rodents down town. It was so disgusting. An old sickly cat/rodent would jump on my head. I couldn't leave all the work to the young Latina women. Then I decided to take three of the little children for a ride. Somehow a black guy ended up driving us. He was a recovering alcoholic and wouldn't turn back. It was dangerous. We were driving in the sand. I called 911.

The image of the cat/rat confusion suggested an undifferentiated complex at the instinctual level. Herbert Rosenfeld, Hannah Segal, and Melanie Klein are British psychoanalysts who wrote about confusional states. According to them, in normal development consistent introjection of the good object provides basic satisfactions of libidinal impulses and eventually leads to a stabilizing core of the ego. This stabilized core is then able to successfully fend off the death instinct. This developmental process leads to the establishment of the stage of normal splitting and the sense of oneself as basically "good." When the immature ego cannot sort out the good object from the bad object, the result is an unhealthy fusion of the death instinct with the life instinct. This means that innate destructiveness is directed at a loved object that is hated and envied for its capacity to excite love, need, and dependency.

Melanie Klein wrote the following about instinctual confusion and its relationship to envy:

> when the fundamental normal splitting into love and hate and into the good and the bad object is not successful, confusion between the good and bad object may arise. I believe this to be the basis of any confusion whether in severe confusional states or in milder forms such as indecision namely a difficulty in coming to conclusions and a disturbed capacity for clear thinking. But confusion is also used defensively: this can be seen on all levels of development. By becoming confused as to whether a substitute for the original figure is good or bad, persecution as well as the guilt about spoiling and attacking the primary object by envy is to some extent counteracted.[8]

The fusion and confusion of old sickly cats and rats that are emerging into view from the unconscious, from below the floorboards, can be understood as the unhealthy fusion of the death instinct (the rats) with the life instinct (the cats) in which the death instinct dominates. It is an image of the psychological condition of this analysand at its most basic and primitive level. It is disgusting to the dreamer, and this unsorted confusion jumps onto her head: it gets into her thoughts and contaminates her ability to think clearly. The emergence of this issue compels the dreamer both to find a solution and to get away from it. As Klein succinctly wrote, confusion is both the condition and a defense against the condition. It creates a psychological emergency to which the dreamer is waking. It is dangerous to continue as she is; it is like driving in the sand. She calls 911 for help.

Confusion and indecision were major issues in the work with this analysand. When a decision needed to be made, the situation became so charged with anxiety and self-persecution that I became alarmed and confused. I was frequently pushed out of an analytic stance into becoming concrete in helping with her dilemmas (i.e., projective identification). Momentarily this shift would bring relief to both of us but was no more than palliative until the next confusional state would arise.

For this analysand, envy had been a longstanding internal dynamic; in the analysis with me, it emerged into our relationship and was enacted between us. Envy in the transference was managed with many defenses in addition to confusional states: it was directed at others, there was idealization of others and me, but especially she turned envious attacks against herself. In my family among my two sisters and mother, envy was rampant and formidable. My defense against envy was to become the "envied" sister, and in this way, I remained unconscious of my own strong envious feelings yet fearful of envious attacks from others. Envy directed at me created a tendency to minimize or denigrate my own achievements in an attempt to protect myself from further envy attacks. Given this history, it was important that I resist the pull of identifying with the role of the "successful" and therefore envied, analyst, as doing so would disconnect me from empathic contact with the painful feelings she needed to learn to feel. The most destructive effects of her envy were toward herself: a denigrating, killing destructiveness that devalued her accomplishments. A *participation mystique* (mutual or reciprocal identification) with her around this painful issue obscured and blurred for some time my ability to be more effective with her in analyzing this complicated dynamic.

Following this dream, I spoke with her about her confusion, when it came up, in terms of how painfully difficult it is to decide what is the best thing to do, and about a pressure inside her that tells her she ought to know *a priori*, what is the right or wrong decision. All this was done bearing in mind that she has a core issue about whether she is fundamentally good. Mostly, I held the knowledge of this core issue in thought and feeling, and this process in me informed my interactions with her. Three months later came a second dream:

> Somehow or other I had a baby RAT! It was supposed to comfort me but it wasn't working. It was always crawling around in the basement playing with the cat. I wanted to get rid of it. A girl (maybe X) said that all you have to do is poison it, but I was afraid the cat might eat the poison also. The cat was beautiful and belonged to Y [an older woman much admired by the dreamer]. So, the girl began to feed the rat poison by hand. It was terrible watching the rat gradually die. I spent a lot of time justifying my need to kill it. A child had been watching and his Father wanted an explanation! I got around it by telling him that I was teaching taxidermy. So I thought the child could see the rat stuffed and preserved. When I looked at it I realized it had turned into a fish, a golden fish, but it was still wiggling a little.

This dream suggests the beginning separation of the cat and the rat. The rat is now a baby rat, a young life, and it is playing. I thought that the image of "play" pointed to a growing recognition that there might be something useful in knowing about her envious destructive parts and a growing capacity to think about them. We spoke more frequently about internal envy attacks that attempt to undermine even small achievements. She still wants to get rid of the problem, and the girl, X, has a simple solution, to poison it. The dreamer is aware that while a differentiation needs to be made, she is fearful that the beautiful cat, that is, the "good object," might be killed as well. Her concern has a transference implication. At that time, I had cats and this analysand has seen them outside my house. Early in the analysis, she expressed "suspiciousness" of cats; she thought they skulked around observing things with malevolent intent. She was naturally suspicious of me. A crucial underlying question was: would I be destructive toward her as was her own malignantly narcissistic and envious mother?

These two dreams indicated that a major piece of primitive shadow material (envy), indicated by the rats, was pushing up for recognition and assimilation. This process brings about intense anxiety. Indeed, when major shadow work is at hand, the old house, the psychic attitudes we live in deteriorate. The rat as the spoiling nasty aspect of our human nature, denigrating the achievements of others, is bad enough. But this nastiness worked against herself as well, spoiling and denigrating her own achievements and inhibiting forward movement.

In the second dream, the figure of the girl, X, was, according to the dreamer's associations, undeveloped, but for whom the dreamer felt affection and motherly concern. While the girl's solution is simplistic, "just poison the rat," it also points to a possible solution. This girl, representing the undeveloped potential of the dreamer, becomes the main active figure in the dream. She gives the rat a drastic remedy, poison. The other side of poison is panacea. In alchemy, the *aqua vitae*, the water of life that quickens and heals is called "poison and panacea." The analytic method itself is poison to some people and life bringing to others, and this can be true for the same individual at different times. This was especially true for this analysand. After one session, she might feel particularly good, feeling as if the analysis were a "saving grace." After another session, she might feel fragmented, angered, and discouraged by something I said and desperate to get away from analysis altogether.

The focus of attention in the dream is upon the rat that is getting the "remedy." Killing in dreams can indicate violent repression, but it can also indicate a painful but necessary sacrifice for there to be a significant transformation. The guilty feelings stirred up by killing the rat can refer to the difficulty in dis-identifying from a malignant complex. It feels so alive—how can one kill a living thing—even if it is destroying you? There is a suggestion as to the goal of this "treatment," which is the transformation of the rat into a living golden fish. In this alchemical change, the rat as the dark, dense *prima materia*, is subjected to multiple procedures to bring about the miraculous "treasure hard to attain," the golden fish.

The alchemists wrote that the most difficult part of the alchemical process is to find the *prima materia*, the material upon which the work is done. This means psychologically that it is difficult to locate the particular issues upon which to work to bring about the most change.

While there is more that could be said about these dreams and the complexities inherent in envy, I want to emphasize that the understanding of envy and its relationship to confusional states brought a specificity of understanding to shadow material as it emerged. It helped me to locate and understand the *prima materia* as it expressed itself in the transference and the countertransference. I was able to work more effectively with her confusion and envy and to unlock the dynamic of negative *coniunctio* to release healthy libido, but it was not without the necessity to revisit my own unworked envy complex. There were times when the *participation mystique* between us felt like we had both taken a bite from Snow White's apple.

Sadomasochism

It is to be expected that there will be passing phases of sadomasochism in any depth analytic work; however, it may be constellated in the analytic relationship in such a way as to be another example of a negative *coniunctio*. As with envy, analysis is a "set-up" for sadomasochism or perhaps better expressed, analysis simply is a sadomasochistic activity from the beginning: the *prima materia* of unconscious complexes must be "tortured" into transformation. Analysis can feel like a sadistic activity to the analysand who is identified with his neurosis or complexes.

The term "sadism" refers to pleasure derived from inflicting pain or humiliation upon another; it derives from the 18th-century writer Marquis de Sade. The term "masochism" refers to pleasure in receiving pain and derives from the 19th-century writer Leopold von Sacher-Masoch. "Sadism" and "masochism" were distinct terms coined by Richard von Krafft-Ebing when he introduced them into medical terminology in 1890. Freud and psychoanalysis joined the terms together as "sadomasochism" because they were viewed as two aspects of a single dynamic. Over the years psychoanalytic writers have had the most to say about sadomasochism, while Jung and writers in analytical psychology, with a few exceptions, have written little on the topic. Writers in the field of clinical psychology and the general population consider sadomasochism to be aberrant, pathological, and perverted.

Case Material

My interest in this topic developed because of an analysis with a man in his mid-40s who, when he first came to see me, had fallen in love with his "dominatrix" and was on the verge of leaving his 16-year marriage. His marriage was loving but nonsexual, and during this time he regularly visited mistresses or "doms" from whom he experienced "complete release and bliss" from subjugation and whippings. It was a secret life that complemented his life as an accomplished professional and loving husband. He and his wife were best friends, but she knew nothing of his secret life and the deep satisfaction it brought to him. He feared she would not understand, be hurt, and condemn him if he revealed it to her. He had seen his current "dom" regularly for the past two years. Recently he and his "dom" had traveled together and discovered deeper feelings for each other than the professional relationship of "pro-dom" to "client-sub" (i.e., the submissive role).

I was transfixed by his story, but my reaction was that he had fallen into an illusory belief that he could transform his current S&M "play" relationship into a "real" relationship in which an S&M component would be integrated into his daily life. I thought to gently dissuade him from his illusion, but with equal force, I had a surprising and powerful reaction that he was on the brink of a "creative catastrophe." His current life, as he described it, seemed exceedingly constricted and compartmentalized. While there was friendship with his wife, there was no sexuality, no real intimacy, and little depth of emotional contact. It struck me that he and his wife had built a safe but sturdy castle for themselves that defended against each other with the illusion to themselves and to the world that all was fine and normal.

This was the beginning of an unconventional analytic relationship. I was drawn into the dynamic of sadomasochism during which I had to analyze my prejudices and my shortsightedness and explore more fully the territory of my own sadomasochism. Later I understood that the excitement about a "creative catastrophe" applied to me, as well. I was drawn into an S&M emotional field: I experienced an uncanny excitement about watching him suffer when his self-built Bastille came crashing down.

As predicted, the decision to tell his wife precipitated a lengthy period of anguish for my analysand. Within a week of separating from his wife, he became so fearful and guilty that he returned to her quite suddenly, leaving the girlfriend stunned, hurt, and mystified. When the wife learned of his need for sessions of humiliation and whippings, she decided he was a sex addict, was mentally ill, and needed a specialist to cure him. She found a psychologist and urged him to make an appointment. But within days of being barraged by her moralistic attitude, he once again moved out of the marital house and went to live with his dominatrix girlfriend.

Telling his wife about his secret life destroyed the carefully erected barriers that kept his sadomasochism sequestered in the "blissful" S&M play sessions with his dominatrix. Sadomasochism began to be felt as an internal dynamic and became enacted in earnest between him and his wife.

During the many years of his split life, he was able to hide from himself how abnormal he felt and how ashamed he was. Now he was consciously face to face with self-loathing about his pathology and aberrant needs. He came to admit and feel disgusted at his needs in just the way his wife expressed when she ranted at him through long e-mails and phone messages. At times he believed she was correct. He felt beat up by her rants and felt that he thoroughly deserved them.

As his analyst, I was subject to a roller coaster of emotions and self-questioning. Had I colluded with myself, or with him, to leave his comfortable marriage? Had I encouraged him out of a voyeuristic tendency in myself? It looked like a disaster: he had unleashed more than he could handle, and I hadn't stopped him. Did I read more creative potential into the situation out of my fascination (*participation mystique*) with the case?

He longed to return to the comfort of his marriage, but that "paradise" was open only if he would renounce his "perverted" ways and submit to deprogramming. Meanwhile, the longed-for paradise with his dom-girlfriend crumbled with every new piece of reality. In the chaos of his crumbled life, he began to feel and name his feelings. He learned about anger, sadness, guilt, grief, longing, and love. In attempting to resolve the reality that the new relationship could not work, they went to a couples' therapist to work out a painful separation. Instead, they began to talk and to listen to each other. An agonizing encounter between two complicated human beings began to happen in earnest, and bonds began to form, of genuine feeling and love.

The next months and years were not smooth going. There were times when they both wanted to shed any remains of their S&M play connection in a shared fantasy of being a "normal couple." In my countertransference, I *also* wished for them to transform completely into "normal" sexual partners, but the strength of their S&M connection was undeniable. In her role as Mistress of the Dungeon, she was in touch with a potent force in herself, a kind of "goddess energy"; in his role as submissive, he found satisfaction that can only be described as a profound religious experience. Some aspects of the S&M dynamic demand to be lived concretely and seemingly could not be analyzed away. I wondered at the lack of my analytic skills or if there was something more to the tenacity of the sadomasochistic phenomenon. I had been dimly aware that his masochism was refractory to analysis indicated by his too-easy compliance in the analysis. Despite my best attempts, I played something of a "dom-pro" to his "client-sub." In this way, we enacted the dynamic rather than subjecting it to analysis.

Gradually it became difficult for my analysand and his new partner to sustain the illusion of a dominant mistress and submissive slave during their play sessions. He knew she was helpless in many basic areas of life; she knew he was a powerful and independent man in his professional life. These realities bled into the pure fantasies of S&M play. Eventually, they become more involved with other couples and with the community living the BDSM (bondage, discipline/dominance, sadism, masochism) lifestyle.

Psychological Dynamics

If we open up the complex emotional state that goes by the word "masochism," we see that it is the experience of suffering for something or someone other than ourselves. This may be voluntary and other times be forced upon one. Motherhood is a voluntary masochistic state. But for infants and children, suffering is inherent in the condition of being small and helpless to the whims of others. In adulthood one may choose to submit and suffer to a greater purpose, for the family, for the love of someone or as devotion, or for a deity. There may or may not be pleasure in this. If one considers masochism from this point of view, it becomes apparent that any development, be it an individual or collective, could not happen without submitting to a painful experience. Empathy, compassion, and love are sometimes subtle derivatives of masochism.

If we open up the complex emotional state we call "sadism," we see it as the ability to be cruel, mean, and cold and the ability to force the submission of someone to one's will. Cruelty and masochism appear to be inborn tendencies and, therefore, in our Jungian language, are archetypal. Melanie Klein regularly observed sadism and cruelty in the play of children as evidence of an observable "death instinct."

But equally sadism can be viewed as a methodology of discovering oneself and the world. How strong am I? How effective am I? Can I force another into submission? What happens when I hurt another? A derivative of cruelty is discipline as when one must be cruel to parts of oneself or another person to reach a goal or realize a specific purpose or to gain mastery over something, oneself, or another.

Masochism and sadism are recognizable as inherent aspects of what Jung called the "religious instinct," a way of expressing the instinct behind the urge to integration and individuation. It is the search for meaning and connection to something beyond the ego. All major religions have as a basis the restraint of pleasure and self-serving instincts in order to make visible an instinct for so-called spiritual development. I suggest that sadomasochism is the basis of the religious instinct: the ability to be cruel to one part of human functioning and to suffer for another part, in the service of something we have traditionally called integration and "wholeness."

As a correlate I suggest that sadomasochism is the basis of the analytic relationship. The acronym BDSM is the preferred rubric for individuals who are living the lifestyle of S&M; within this acronym are three pairings: bondage and discipline, dominance and submission, sadism and masochism.

When an analytic relationship takes hold, there is an implicit aspect of *bondage and discipline*. Transference creates bondage and makes it difficult to break away from analysis without doing psychic damage. Analysis requires discipline to look at fantasies and dreams for the meaning they may reveal and discipline against anything that might sidetrack or seduce away from the analytic tasks at hand.

Dominance and submission. Both the analyst and the analysand submit to the process of analysis, but the dynamic occurs between them as well. The analysand submits to the analytic process, but so does the analyst. If the analyst holds herself aloof and outside the process, as a superior being, then the work goes awry or does not work at all.

These pairings are easily identifiable as part of a spiritual or religious practice and in an analytic relationship. Perhaps less so with the last pairing, *sadism and masochism*. But if one is sensitive to primitive emotions that are generated in analysis, one will experience the back-and-forth play of masochism and sadism between the analyst and the analysand. Like in the play of children, an analysis must continually discover and rediscover the nature of *this* particular analysis. There is a reliving of childhood emotions that serves the creative play of individuation in the analytic encounter. This aspect interests me most because it has the potential to bring depth and vitality and to be highly creative.

For example, Ms. X felt her analyst was being deliberately sadistic toward her by keeping the temperature in the consulting room too cold. Analyst Y became masochistic when he allowed the temperature to be uncomfortable for him to accommodate Ms. X. Ms. X tormented analyst Y with accusations of his being sadistic while doing so in a sadistic manner. Ms. X felt masochistic through feelings of being caught and was unable to escape the analysis. These were very real, uncomfortable, and troubling emotions.

Mr. A felt his analyst was being deliberately cruel by withholding valuable insights and help, doling them out slowly, one at a time, session after session. Analyst B felt that Mr. A was sadistic by withholding his thoughts, feelings, and associations during sessions giving analyst B nothing to work with. Both Mr. A and Analyst B felt in bondage to an emotional struggle from which neither one could escape. Analyst B felt like an inadequate analyst, unable to do her job and wishing Mr. A would just leave and put her out of her misery. Mr. A felt he should stay in the analysis, no matter how painful and frustrating, to force help from an unrelentingly unhelpful parental figure.

In both cases above, there was the inability to discern whether what was happening was an unhealthy, addictive, and defensive process leading nowhere or a process invaluable to the eventual growth and development of both the analysand and the analyst.

As with envy, masochism and sadism are archetypal; they are basic to the human condition and play important roles in the development of the individual and human culture. As a linked dynamic, sadomasochism forms a core aspect of the *coniunctio oppositorum*. However, this dynamic as an archetypal dynamism can become constellated as a defense and lead to a negative *coniunctio* and a negative therapeutic reaction. Bion described a phenomenon he called "reversible perspective."[9] An example is when good interpretations are seemingly taken in by the ego, but later the analyst discovers that these interpretations have been taken up by a harsh superego that uses the interpretations in a sadistic way against the ego. Instead of the ego making good use of "analytic food" in the service of growth and development, the analysis turns into a defensive cycle of S&M. This is a negative *coniunctio*, as no growth or development issues from that dynamic. Bion wrote that a pattern of "reversible perspective" might go on for a long time without notice.

My experience and reflections have led me to see that sadomasochism is present in all relationships, analytic or otherwise, although it is certainly stronger or more obvious in some.

An analysand was on the brink of beginning what felt to be a self-destructive, masochistic relationship; she remarked to me, "I feel like there is a glass of poison in front of me and I cannot stop myself from drinking it." It became a difficult, trying, and at times parasitic and addictive relationship, but it was also enlivening pushing her far beyond what she thought she could tolerate. Through minute and careful tracking of her emotional states in session after session, she gradually worked her way through this precarious territory.

I want to emphasize that the negative *coniunctio* is not necessarily to be avoided. The question is, for example, whether a sadomasochistic relationship can eventually be put to good use. Perhaps the analytic process gets driven into it; as if through a repetition compulsion, the process seeks something vital, deep, alive, and creative. The knowledge that one must be close to the toxin to be vitally creative, psychologically awake, and alive is well known among artists. Eschewing easy answers and well-worn patterns of life may be a necessary path for many analyses and certainly for many vital relationships. In this manner, the negative *coniunctio* becomes a necessary *via negativa*.

Sadomasochism in Films

Films are a useful medium for the psychoanalyst to learn more about the difficult emotional territory of sadomasochism. Two films, *Secretary* and *The Night Porter*, portray a sadomasochistic relationship. They attempt to penetrate deeper into the S&M phenomenon and push against the limits of conventional dictums and constraints as if to search for something hidden within. In very different settings they portray characters that are adaptive to the conventions and expectations in which they live. The price they pay is a lost connection to what is felt to be life sustaining.

In *Secretary*[10] Lee Holloway has a history of cutting and other self-destructive behavior that culminates in a suicide attempt. Her father is an out-of-control, disingenuous alcoholic; her mother and sister are well intentioned but superficial. Lee suffers from a lack of connection to an authentic sense of herself. After being released from the hospital, she obtains her first job as a secretary to an eccentric lawyer, Mr. E. Edward Grey.

In the first several scenes, Mr. Grey makes an impact on Miss Holloway. He challenges her innocent persona and questions her secrecy and her cutting; she responds and is able to take him in, and she begins to change. He senses her masochistic leanings that bring out his sadism. Miss Holloway challenges the schizoid shell of Mr. Grey. The back-and-forth process between them sharpens. Previously each had been locked in an internally corrosive, self-destructive pattern. They had been asleep to the truth, that they were more dead than alive. But now they bring these patterns to bear upon each other. They begin a sadomasochistic relationship in which he spanks her, berates her, and tells her what to do. He awakens her and then she "retaliates" by challenging him to abandon his shamed, isolated state. But he cannot bear the aliveness that she awakens in him, his feelings, and especially his love for her. So he fires her and sends her away.

Lee temporarily regresses to her former state of passivity and compliance. As she makes preparations to marry her old boyfriend, Peter, a new life possibility quickens inside her, and she takes action. She runs back to Mr. Grey and asserts that they can be together in a 24/7 S&M relationship. At first Mr. Grey rebuffs her, but then he puts her to the test; he orders her to sit at the desk until he returns, which he does two days later.

In *The Night Porter*[11] Lucia is the glamorous wife of a famous music conductor when she encounters Max, a night porter working at an upscale hotel in Vienna. It is many years after the end of WWII, and both are living seemingly normal, adapted lives. From their first glance when they see each other, they are drawn to remember themselves in a dark, survival relationship that took place during the war in a Nazi prison camp. Back then they were locked in an intensely loving but sadomasochistic relationship. It was a "bigger than life" connection and a way of surviving the depraved "lesser than life" environment of the death camp.

Lucia and Max at first try to sidestep the pull to be with each other again, after all those years. They are repulsed but drawn by the power of their past connection; they resist and fight the toxin that has surfaced. They attempt to hate each other, to drive each other away, to get rid of the strength of their compulsion.

The power of the call to life beyond death pulls them together into a violent, demonic *coniunctio* that has no way out. There is no cure for them, Lucia tells someone in another scene. There is no cure for their experience together in the prison camps—only each other—poison and panacea are absolutely one, fused together in one deadly mix. Unable to obtain food and sought by former Nazis, Lucia and Max become isolated with no option but death. Upon reaching the point of starvation, Max carries Lucia outside early one morning; they walk onto a bridge and are killed by their enemies.

One aspect of the negative *coniunctio* is that it appears to be and feels to be a "no-win" situation. Wilfred Bion described the challenge with experiences of "nothing" or "no-thing."[12] If whatever is felt to be missing, or not there, can be held mentally rather than be evacuated, via projective identification, then the "no-thing" becomes a thought, and an apparatus for thinking it by necessity develops. Repeated experiences, of tolerating the frustration of the "no-thing," lead to psychological growth.

My analysand, who felt she was about to drink poison, would at times say there was "nothing" for her in that relationship, but it became a "no-thing" experience that initiated her into what the poet John Keats described as "negative capability." Bion picked up this notion from Keats to describe the ability to tolerate one's own experience of ignorance in the forms of uncertainty, mystery, and doubt. Without this capability, the experience of "nothing" is unbearable, cannot be put to good use, and is usually got rid of by some form of compulsive acting out.

The Night Porter shows a disturbing, regressive pull to a "no way out" situation, no way out except to death. But is this the only perspective? Lucia seemed aware when she stated that there is no cure for her, nor for Max; she implied they were making a choice. A choice not to live was felt to be more alive and preferable to living in a state of mental and emotional death. Those few last days together, in many ways, completed their lives.

However, where *The Night Porter* fails to escape the drive toward parasitic, mutual self-destruction, *Secretary* portrays characters who are able to make use of the experience, who move away from an unwholesome fusion of life and death instincts to an assertion of the life instinct between them that vitalizes and cures them both.

There are many comparisons to make between the relationship depicted in *Secretary* and the relationship that is depicted in *The Night Porter*. And of course, they are very different films. *Secretary* was billed as a quirky, dark comedy while *The Night Porter* was a pessimistic, even pornographic film noir. In the latter, Lucia and Max fall into the power of sadomasochism in which thinking and feeling are obliterated by blind compulsion; whereas in *Secretary*, internal compulsions are made conscious through the medium of relationship. In *The Night Porter*, we see a relentless descent into a deadly *coniunctio*. In *Secretary*, Miss Holloway and Mr. Grey negotiate the pull of the negative *coniunctio* and are able to make use of the addictive aspects in the service of a new, healthy reality.

These films are meant to touch difficult emotional states in the viewer. As examples of extreme *contra naturam*, they challenge our comfort, crack us open, and touch places where we are still innocent to disturbing psychic realities.

Conclusion

A major question within psychoanalysis is: what causes or circumstances create or bring about the negative *coniunctio* in any of its various patterns? This question can be answered in roughly two ways. Relational traumas in childhood in which good internal objects either are not developed (introjected) or have become lost are the cause of many perverse, destructive internal psychodynamic patterns. The other answer lies in the nature of the psyche itself described as having aggressive and destructive instincts that require continual modification. There may be considerable overlap and application of both points of view.

Analytical psychology considers the above question but in addition might ask, "What for?" It seems hardly possible to think there is anything "for" to be asked about when the goal of an analysis of such cases is to restore and promote a creative, meaningful, and productive life. Are these examples merely aberrant patterns? Is there anything inherently valuable in the negative *coniunctio*?

I suggest that the negative *coniunctio* broadens and pushes the boundaries of what is normative. We see in cases, in which a negative *coniunctio* turns, transforms, and becomes productive and creative, that the entire process brings about a widening and deepening of consciousness, a transformed psyche that is more vital. Because the negative *coniunctio* is a specific example of *participation mystique*, the analyst becomes intimately involved with and affected by the negative *coniunctio* dynamic, subject to the same widening and deepening effects as the patient.

Psychoanalysis is continually asked to experience and reformulate the nature of both the psyche and psychoanalysis itself. There is an ongoing need to recognize and explore these patterns of the *coniunctio* that may only appear dark and negative because they remain in the shadows.

Notes

1 Haruki Murakami, *What I Talk About When I Talk About Running* (New York: Random House, 2008), 96.
2 Jung, *Psychology of the Transference*, CW 16, para. 355.
3 Donald Meltzer, *Sexual States of Mind* (Perthshire, Scotland: Clunie Press, 1973), 98.
4 Sigmund Freud, *Beyond the Pleasure Principle, SE 18* (London: Hogarth Press, 1920).
5 Sigmund Freud, *The Ego and the Id, SE 19* (London: Hogarth Press, 1923).
6 Wilfred Bion, *Attention and Interpretation* (London: Karnac, 1970), 95.
7 Edward Edinger, *Anatomy of the Psyche* (LaSalle, IL: Open Court, 1985), 211.
8 Melanie Klein, *Envy and Gratitude* (New York: Basic Books, 1957), 62.
9 Wilfred Bion, *Elements of Psycho-Analysis* (London: Karnac, 1963), 50–63.
10 Steven Shainberg, director. *Secretary*, Lionsgate Films, 2002.
11 Liliana Cavani, director. *The Night Porter*, Ital-Noleggio Cinematografico, 1974.
12 Wilfred Bion, *Learning From Experience* (London: Karnac, 1962), 34.

Chapter 6

Distillation of "Feeling Values" in Turbulent Times

Introduction

The genesis of this chapter was the US presidential election of 2016. Sensing momentous changes at hand, I paid attention to books, films, and music that came out during and around the time of the election. I was reminded that during difficult times, for both the collective and the individual, there can be heightened creative output. I gave a presentation of works that drew my attention, to point out what I thought were emerging "new feeling values" forced by the pressure of a tumultuous time. However, it is the nature of humans to be creative in relation to and reaction to events in the larger world. One role of art is to metabolize the challenges of whatever is the current world situation. This essay is based mostly on that original presentation but has broader and ongoing implications. "Feeling values" are continually being generated, and then there may be a reaction against them. I think notably of the flowering of German expressionism during the early 20th century only to be denounced as degenerate art by the Nazis in a notorious exhibition in 1937.

Dmitri Shostakovich

The Noise of Time, a novel by British author Julian Barnes, based on the life of the composer Dmitri Shostakovich was published in January 2016.[1] The Russian composer was in mid-stride of a promising music career, having composed three symphonies, and working on his fourth when, in January of 1936, Joseph Stalin came to see a performance of his opera *Lady Macbeth of Mtsensk*, which had received critical acclaim around the world since its premiere in 1934. After Stalin's visit, an editorial appeared in the official government mouthpiece, *Pravda*, with the headline, "Muddle instead of Music." The opera was roundly denounced as not in line with the agenda of Soviet art, and its popularity around the world was further proof that the work pandered to the taste of the bourgeois West. The *Pravda* editorial *shook* Shostakovich as it was a crushing blow to his developing musical talent. A few years later, such a pronouncement would mean exile or literal death.

DOI: 10.4324/9781003434009-7

After our presidential election of November 2016, I thought much about Shostakovich given that we were about to enter a dramatically different, unknown, and perhaps frightening period in US history. I pondered the relationship between art and the context of its time. Context is many things: personal, geographic, and historical and can be an opportunity and a limitation. Ludwig Beethoven's limitation was going deaf early in his life and being deaf for the last years of his life. Shostakovich's limitation was to be living and composing in Russia during the time of Stalin.

Adverse circumstances and severe limitations can bring about extraordinary creative achievements. I cannot imagine, for example, the late period of Beethoven's music being possible without his being deaf. Withdrawn into his interior world, he created a musical language that reached a dimension most likely not possible without profound hearing loss. Do artists reach a certain level of artistry despite adversity, because of it, or perhaps with little or no relationship at all? In the end, the work of art, the symphony, the painting, the book, or the movie must stand on its own apart from context. This is because good art, while requiring talent, skill, and hard work, has a crucial element that is not consciously contrived, and which transcends context.

After the harsh rebuke by the state government, Shostakovich was faced with the dilemma of abandoning his musical development or finding a different occupation. He withdrew his 4th symphony, which was already in rehearsals, and after a period of time, began work on a 5th symphony. It premiered in the fall of 1937 and was met with much applause and approval by the government. A subsequent article appeared in *Pravda* that described the 5th symphony as "a Soviet Artist's creative reply to just criticism." Shostakovich was credited with having written that statement, something he never repudiated. Some scholars believe he did *not* write it but allowed it to stand as a cover under which he could continue to compose.

Understanding the 5th symphony has varied over the years with the underlying question: did Shostakovich cave in or not? Many people favor a dark irony in this and his later works sensing that he discovered a way to compose music from a level that would escape notice by the Kremlin. In his memoir (he died in 1975), Shostakovich wrote that composing during the years of Soviet terror was "as if someone were beating you with a stick and saying, 'your business is rejoicing, your business is rejoicing.'" Whether one regards this symphony as veiled anguish or upbeat and rejoicing, it "continues to be regarded as a major achievement."[2]

In February and March of 2017, the St Petersburg Philharmonic was on tour in the USA playing this 5th symphony so that, as one reviewer wrote, people could judge for themselves Shostakovich's intent. The last movement is upbeat and bombastic seemingly intent upon leaving no doubt in the superficial listener's mind that Shostakovich was doing the "business of rejoicing." To another listener, one might hear the composer "being beaten," under all that bombast.

The original score of the shelved 4th Symphony was lost during the war and rediscovered by the Philharmonic librarian in 1961. It was performed 25 years to the date it was originally scheduled. Shostakovich, still alive, was delighted by the resurrection of his 4th, a gargantuan, heavily Mahler-influenced work. But some critics note that, in the end, Shostakovich might have been well served by the Stalinist-era crackdown on the modernist tendencies in Soviet music. Whether it shaped the power of his music to better ends remains an open question.

Moonlight

The movie *Moonlight*[3] was released late in 2016, just prior to the election. It was described as a coming-of-age story of a black gay man, named Chiron, growing up in the gang drug culture of Miami. Yes, it is all those things, shown at three different periods of his life. One feels empathy for him being raised by a drug-addicted mother, left alone, bullied at school, and later, beaten up for being gay. There are conventional tropes to manipulate one's feelings throughout the film. But the quieter moments feel the most real, the best of the film, the most contemporary, and what moves the film into the realm of something new. The space, the words not spoken, but felt. The film portrays a hopeful human connection. Not sentimental, not tragic, not violent, just real, the way things are, the way things can be.

Noteworthy are the scenes between Juan, the drug dealer, and the young boy Chiron. Juan reaches out and talks to Chiron, man to man, as an equal. In the "baptismal scene," Juan teaches Chiron how to be comfortable in the water and to swim. The music that frames this baptismal scene is classical music to which "chopped and screwed," a technique derived from Southern hip-hop music, has been applied.

Later, the young Chiron confronts Juan by asking him if he sells dope to his mother. Juan doesn't sidestep the truth but steps into the issue and owns it. And when Chiron asks Juan about the meaning of the word "faggot," Juan tells him that the word is used to make someone feel bad about himself. It is real communication done with care, respect, and honesty.

Juan is gone for the second part replaced by his best friend, Kevin with whom he has his first sexual experience. In the third part, near the end of the film, Kevin reaches out to Chiron after their lives have gone different ways for many years. Kevin calls him up after hearing a piece of music, and then Chiron drives to visit Kevin at the café where he works as a short-order cook. Later they go to Kevin's apartment. It is a quiet, moving, and slow-moving scene in which small gestures carry a wealth of emotion and genuine feeling. In the last scene of the film, when Kevin, striped of pretensions, not having seen Chiron for several years, gently confronts him about his appearance. Chiron has "fronts," metallic teeth coverings that gang members wear. He is unlike the Chiron he knew as a teenager. Keven gently reminds Chiron of who he really is, a gentle and vulnerable soul who wants tender love.

Moonlight is full of moments that display that we have moved beyond the individual, to a recognition of the truth to be discerned *within* human contact. The questions are: Who am I in this world today? Who am I behind the props, slogans, and labels with which I want to identify?

Arrival

The movie *Arrival*,[4] based on a short story by Ted Chiang,[5] was also released late in 2016, just after the presidential election. It is a sci-fi film, which, despite numerous clichés, allows intellectual complexity and emotional richness to dominate.

Louise Banks, a linguist, has been brought in to decode the language and to make contact with aliens, called Heptapods (they have seven "feet") that have arrived in large spacecraft that hover above Earth. As Louise begins to understand the aliens, she is affected by them and begins to experience an alteration in her perception of time. The interpenetration of future and present increasingly affects her consciousness throughout the rest of the film.

Noticing the canary in the cage was hopping around, breathing easily, Louise Banks takes off her protective suit and headgear so that the aliens can see her and she can better see them. She submits herself to direct contact, to learn why they are here. One can tell from the outset that she has a different feeling for Abbot and Costello, the two Heptapods, than do her superiors. She embraces them and wants to understand and be understood by them. She firmly confronts the restrictive and insular mindsets of the scientists and military people who dangerously misunderstand the simple process of "getting to know someone." Her receptivity to the Heptapods allows her to begin to think like them and to learn that time is different for them, that the past and future are all part of one reality, here in the present. From this knowledge and despite knowing fully what the future will bring, when the physicist, her love interest, later suggests that they "make a baby," she embraces him and their future life for the joy and the heart-wrenching sorrow that it will bring.

Kendrick Lamar

Kendrick Lamar is an outstanding artist among hip-hop rappers. He was born and grew up in Compton, California, during the time that the first generation of West Coast rappers were at work: Dr. Dre, Easy E, Ice Cube, and the group forming NWA. He experienced firsthand the gangs and drug culture in which he lived. He began rapping as a teen and has received critical acclaim for several albums. His album, DAMN, was released in April of 2017, just before he turned 30. It has received many awards, most recently the Pulitzer Prize, and is considered one of the finest Rap albums to date.

I began to study hip-hop music after I saw the movie *Straight Outta Compton*,[6] released in 2015. At first, I admired the rappers more than I enjoyed them. Rap music has been a transformative force in music. As the rapper Jay-Z said, "It provides a gateway to conversations that normally would not be had."[7] First, an organizing force within black culture, DJ-ing and rapping have now extended all over the world. *Every* culture has some form of rapping, a form that was developed first by Jamaican musicians in the South Bronx. The East Coast School was met by the West Coast School of rapping, and the war between them culminated in the deaths of the seminal rappers Tupac Shakur and Biggie Smalls in the late 1900s.

After the heavy gangster rap of the 1990s, the current expression has become emotionally and psychologically complex. The music remains violent and assaultive, which I take as one of the points. "Get it? See what it feels like!" as a kind of projective identification received by me, a white woman living in upscale Santa Monica, just 25 miles north of Compton, in a vastly different world. There's a documentary called *Streets of Compton*[8] in which someone asks a little kid sitting in the corner what he wants to do when he grows up. He says he wants to be a rapper and begins to freestyle his rhymes on the spot. That goal has become a possible escape from the no-win context of drugs and gang life in places like Compton.

In the music video of the song "DNA,"[9] Kendrick Lamar, in handcuffs, is in dialogue with his interrogator, Don Cheadle. Lamar questions and asserts his identity as a black man as he raps about his paradoxical nature. The voice that comes out of Don Cheadle is also Lamar's voice. Hearing the rapid back and forth between Cheadle and Lamar, the listener is inducted into the painful, frustrating rage and complexity of the black man's experience in America.

In October 2019, in Minneapolis, Minnesota, I gave a presentation about the history and development of Rap music, from the birth of hip hop in August of 1973, playing music video clips from the early pioneers, Biggie Smalls, Grandmaster Flash, and Jay-Z, to the West Coast rap scene including NWA. I followed those with clips of Rap music videos from Africa, Brazil, Afghanistan, and Sweden to demonstrate the movement of a musical genre around the world. I discovered that every country, without exception, has some kind of Rap scene and that the simple mix of beats with sung or spoken poetry became an art form that expressed similar sentiments. I was excited to share my discoveries with a group of mostly white, middle-class Jungian analysts and candidates, most of whom didn't know much about the history of hip-hop and rap.

It didn't go very well. There was considerable pushback about music "that wasn't easy to dance to" that "felt aggressive," "had a lot of swear words," and in general was just unpleasant. I was stunned. Having immersed myself in Rap music for several years, I wanted the audience to see and feel Rap music as a genuine art form and to appreciate what had emerged from the black, Afro-American culture that decided, one hot August summer evening, to throw a block party for *themselves*. This is an example of artistic expression emerging from difficult times, of new "feeling values" being created from "nothing" and by some very creative minds. My audience, with a few exceptions, wasn't having it. I felt like I had failed with my presentation.

Things changed a few months later when in May 2020, in the same city, Minneapolis, the killing of George Floyd set off a major racial upheaval all over the USA. Suddenly, NWA's aggressive "Straight Outta Compton" and "F**k the Police!" found resonance. In 2021, in Los Angeles, I did a longer presentation on Rap music that included many music video clips. This time, the reception was different.

Years Later

As we in the USA prepare for another election round, political polarities have increased, mass shootings are an everyday news item, the weather is catastrophic everywhere, and AI (artificial intelligence) is being greeted with decidedly mixed reactions. What I wrote in the first part of this chapter remains true. Artistic expressions in music, TV shows, and contemporary art play a part in metabolizing the seemingly undigestible nature of our world. As an example, the TV series *Atlanta*[10] created by the multi-gifted Donald Glover over four seasons from 2016 to 2022 expresses a potent sensibility of Afro-Surrealism and sardonic collisions between white and black culture.

We don't live in an extreme totalitarian state like Stalin's Soviet Union. But we have discovered without a doubt that we do not live in a post-racial world. Nor do we live in a world with broad acceptance of multi-cultural, multi-gender values. The truth has been exposed in a kind of apocalyptic uncovering: the intensity of bigotry, racism, and intolerance; selfish and mean-spirited interests of politicians, governments, and companies have been starkly exposed and have revealed the illusion presented by a naive belief in a democratic process and progressive liberal values.

We live in a world of fear, trauma, and loss of innocence. The individual is swamped by news information and social media, which have become dark and destructive. Increasing connectivity implies and creates dispersal and dissolution that lead to pseudo-connectivity: the belief that we are connected when, really, we are not.

Our media age presents a challenge for the traditional Jungian perspective. Not only is authentic individual development becoming a more difficult enterprise, but there is also an additional challenge as part of our post-postmodern era. How do we go through and beyond the value of Jungian individuation? It may no longer be the question of how one fully realizes oneself through a relationship to the depths of the psyche. In addition, how does one face the truth of our time and in relation to that truth, how can one feel and think as deeply as possible?

Our own future consciousness is already here as intimations visible on the periphery. It is possible to access it if one can see through the literal and not be blinded by understandable but protective emotional reactions. Perhaps our current disorienting and turbulent times provide impetus toward a leap of consciousness to another level. Any future consciousness involves further development of "impersonal feeling" by which I mean feeling that is not emotion, sentiment, or personal. It is feeling for values.

The philosopher Slavoj Zizek wrote, "The traumatic event represents where the Real disrupts the smooth running of the symbolic."[11] Perhaps the art of our time speaks to this disruption, and our challenge is *not* to push back against the disruption but to meet it and discover new values of thinking and feeling. In this way, we face our turbulent times and cooperate with the work of evolving consciousness.

Postscript: Gregor Samsa

I loved the first lines of Kafka's short story "Metamorphosis" so much that when I learned a little German, I memorized them in the original. "*Als Gregor Samsa eines Morgens aus unruhigen Träumen erwachte, fand er sich in seinem Bett zu einem ungeheureren Ungeziefer verwandelt.*"[12] "When Gregor Samsa awoke from troubled dreams one morning, he found that he had been transformed in his bed into an enormous bug." I love that in German the verb is at the end. It is music with words in the most favorable order. What has happened is right there as the end-of-sentence punctuation. "Die Verwandlung," the transformation, of course, refers to Gregor finding himself turned into a large bug. But there is another way to understand Gregor's transformation. Being a bug was the state in which he had been living, and, one morning, for unknown reasons, this realization came home to him, and he found himself, he discovered himself to be what he really was. What kind of bug we are not definitively informed, but from the descriptions, it is most likely a beetle or some kind. A kind of low-level creature that plays its part—mindlessly—in the life of bug-hood. Gregor was living his life with little self-reflection and at the service of his low-level family system. Even in his changed form, from man to bug, he desires to get to work on time and meet the expectations of his parents and his company. His changed appearance "bugged" his family who couldn't stand the sight of him, except for his sister who brought him food, although the wrong kind. The real metamorphosis was the gradual change from the bug existence he had been living into a sentient, feeling, self-reflecting creature. Shunned and loathed, he died feeling love for the music his sister played. The story doesn't end there. After the bug corpse is disposed of, the family thrives: his sister develops a life for herself, and the father goes back to work as does the mother. When severe limitations are imposed, a transformation is forced to happen. But it can kill you, or it can feel like it is killing you.

Notes

1 Julian Barnes, *The Noise of Time* (New York: Alfred A. Knopf, 2016).
2 Stuart Isacoff, "A Subversive, Symphonic Response to Stalin," *Wall Street Journal*, March 10, 2017, sec. Books and Art.
3 Barry Jenkins, director. *Moonlight*, A24, Camera Film, 2016.
4 Denis Villeneuve, director. *Arrival*, Paramount Pictures, 2016.
5 Ted Chiang, *Stories of Your Life and Others*, 1st ed. (New York: Tor, 2002).
6 F. Gary Gray, director. *Straight Outta Compton*, Universal Pictures, 2015.
7 Zadie Smith, *Feel Free: Essays* (New York: Penguin Books, 2019).
8 Mark Ford, director. *Streets of Compton*, TV documentary. A&E Networks, 2016.
9 https://youtu.be/NLZRYQMLDW4.
10 Donald Glover, creator. *Atlanta* tv series. FX, 2016–2022.
11 Tony Myers, *Slavoj Zizek* (Abingdon, UK: Routledge, 2003), 26.
12 Franz Kafka and Stanley Appelbaum, *Best Short Stories =: Die Schönsten Erzählungen*, A Dual-Language Book (Mineola, NY: Dover Publications, 1997), 24–5.

Chapter 7

Melancholia and Catastrophic Change

An Essay on the Film *Melancholia* (2011)

Prominently in the mind of writer/director Lars von Trier when he developed his film, *Melancholia* (2011), was his own mental state. Struggling with depression, he searched for inspiration for a new project to follow the dark, pornographically violent, nearly unwatchable *Antichrist* (2009). Hearing about how depressives react in the face of a disaster became a seed. "My analyst told me that melancholics will usually be more level-headed than ordinary people in a disastrous situation, partly because they can say: 'What did I tell you?' But also because they have nothing to lose."[1]

Von Trier saw a TV documentary in which he learned that Saturn is the planet for melancholia. He read about cosmic collisions on the Internet, listened to music, and went to museums. He said, "I think Justine is very much me. She is based a lot on my person and my experiences with doomsday prophecies and depression. Whereas Claire is meant to be a normal person."[2]

The film begins with an eight-minute opening sequence of extreme slow-motion images that take one through the story from the beginning to the final swallowing up of Earth by a massive planet. The viewer knows what will eventually occur. Von Trier wants to get the ending out of the way—no distracting suspense. After the opening sequence, the film is divided into two parts. Part one is the reception for Justine's wedding at the elegant estate of her older sister, Claire, and Claire's husband, John. Part two takes place in the aftermath of the wedding reception. Justine has fallen into a severe depressive episode and has come to stay at the estate where Claire is nursing her. At this time a rogue planet called Melancholia is approaching and threatens to collide with Earth. Justine is the first to notice an unusually bright star, and later she notices when it disappears. At the end of *Melancholia*, Justine helps her young nephew Leo gather sticks to make a "magic cave" that will "protect" them. She brings her distraught sister, Claire, with Leo into the structure. The three sit together, holding hands, waiting for the end.

Justine is a depressive personality for whom the ordinary demands of life are too great. She does not know how to participate in life in a meaningful way. She has episodes where she flouts collective expectations. She acts out impulses and creates emotional turbulence with everyone, or she falls into a deep depression, unable to bathe or eat. Food tastes like ashes, and all she wants to do is sleep.

DOI: 10.4324/9781003434009-8

However, Justine is gifted; she "knows" things that others don't, and she senses beyond ordinary reality. But she is unable to use what she knows to benefit herself or to live a creative life, and she always expects the worst to happen. As the disaster approaches, Justine's depression improves. She becomes calm while Claire becomes increasingly anxious.

Claire is caring, loving, more normal, and adapted. But there is a thin quality to her personality, intimations of a life not fully lived. Claire cares deeply for her sister but can make no sense of her. She is disturbed by Justine's erratic behavior. Claire needs life and people to be nice and untroublesome. Eventually, through the sister connection, Claire, too, begins to sense that something is off with the mysterious planet moving closer to Earth. She tries to allow herself to be reassured by her husband but secretly checks out rumors on the Internet that claim Melancholia is in a dance of death with Earth. Claire becomes increasingly anxious because she, in contrast to Justine, has everything to lose: her life, her marriage, and her young son, Leo.

John is the abnormally normal husband of Claire—wealthy, pompous, competent, and sure of himself and his values. An amateur astronomer, he tells everyone that the new planet is no threat. He believes the scientists who assure the public that Melancholia will give Earth an unprecedented, dazzling display as it passes close by. When he realizes he is wrong, he tells his son: "There is nothing to do, there is no place to hide." In the face of this shattering fact, he takes an overdose of sleeping pills and dies in the barn among the horses.

Another major player in this film is the lush, hyperbolic, over-the-top music of the prelude to Wagner's opera *Tristan und Isolde*. The images in the opening scene, which move the viewer through the story of *Melancholia*, are drenched in emotionally evocative, chromatically ambiguous tonalities. After the beginning, the music slips in here and there in the form of judicious intimations and suggestions. It comes fully forward only in a few specific places and, of course, throughout the ending.

Experienced at the level of a literal story, it is difficult not to be moved by the emotional ending. Previously, Justine had been unable to participate meaningfully in any ritual, including her own wedding. Forced into an extreme situation, she is able to create a rite of passage, a meaningful final ritual. All of this is foreshadowed in images from the initial sequence. We, the viewers, know what is to come. Still, it is emotionally wrenching when we finally see it happen.

Justine

After the opening sequence, Justine and her new husband arrive very late to their wedding reception in a stretch limo that moves slowly up a narrow dirt road to the estate. Toasts to the bride and groom are interrupted by Justine's estranged parents' highly charged, vitriolic animosity. Her mother denounces the very idea of marriage while her father sits with several dates, floozies all named "Betty," stuffing spoons into his lapel pocket. The parents steal the moment from the wedding couple, and as they do, Justine disappears into a dissociative state.

As a depressive personality, Justine longs to end it all, to get it all over with—this ridiculous life of disingenuous relationships, values she cannot believe in, and promises that feel vacuous and disgusting to her. She wants to believe her new husband, Michael, can bring her happiness, but this hope falls flat over and over during the wedding reception. Justine attempts to approach and engage her parents. Her mother is walled off in a castle of bitterness and resentment while her father is lost in a haze of self-indulgence and hedonistic womanizing.

We can justifiably infer that Justine's parental relationships left her unprepared to engage with life in a fulfilling and meaningful way. Life and people, once a source of hope, have left her disconnected and filled with despair and disappointment. Not knowing how to repair these gaps in herself, she settled into a pattern of life that left her isolated from herself and others.

Justine tries unsuccessfully to talk with her mother, and she begs her father to stay overnight so they can talk the next day. She needs something, she longs for something, but she does not know what or how to get it. In this vacuum, the planet Melancholia appears on the scene. What Justine longs for is, in Christopher Bollas's terminology, a "transformational object."[3] In the face of not being able to think or feel what she really longs for and being convinced that what she longs for does not exist, she longs for the end. The planet becomes for her a transformational object and, at the same time, synonymous with the end of everything.

The search for the transformational object is the earliest search, according to Bollas, to repair the connection to life that was lost at an early stage of development.

> To seek the transformational object is to recollect an early object experience, to remember not cognitively but existentially—through intense affective experience—a relationship which was identified with cumulative transformational experiences of the self. Its intensity as an object relation is not due to the fact that this is an object of desire, but to the object being identified with such powerful metamorphoses of being.[4]

Justine follows Melancholia's "call" and moves into a psychosomatic fusion with the mysterious planet. During one scene she goes into the woods and lies naked in the planet's light. This is one of the moments when Wagner's music comes forward. The music is an intimation of another world.

> On the occasion of the aesthetic moment . . . an individual feels a deep subjective rapport with an object and experiences an uncanny fusion with the object, an event that re-evokes an ego state that prevailed during early psychic life. . . . This anticipation of being transformed by an object inspires the subject with a reverential attitude towards it, so that even though the transformation of the self will not take place on the scale it reached during early life, the adult subject tends to nominate such objects as sacred.[5]

After her "communion" with Melancholia, Justine is cured. She regains her appetite and her sanity. Meanwhile, everyone around her begins to disintegrate into panic and anxiety. Justine idealizes destructive change; destruction becomes a healing symbol for her. Once she recognizes what is going to happen, she worships the deadly planet and becomes its devotee. She understands that the world is evil and that it deserves to be destroyed. To add distress to despair, she states, in her knowing way, that there is no other life anywhere in the universe. It is all over. Depressive thinking, par excellence! But it is also melancholic thinking, and the giveaway is the moralistic stance Justine takes toward the world—and ultimately, toward herself.

In *Mourning and Melancholia*, Freud lays out the psychology of melancholy. He writes that both normal mourning and melancholy begin with the loss of an object. The loss can be literal, as in death, but can include "all those situations of being slighted, neglected or disappointed."[6] In the condition of melancholy, the process of grieving and mourning goes awry. The libidinal cathexis of the lost object is not withdrawn and placed onto another object, as is the case with normal mourning. In melancholy, this libido is withdrawn into the ego and serves

> to establish an identification of the ego with the abandoned object. Thus the shadow of the object fell upon the ego, and the latter could henceforth be judged by a special agency [the superego], as though it were an object, the forsaken object.[7]

An intrapsychic sadomasochistic activity takes place in which the superego berates, debases, and abuses the ego "making it suffer and deriving sadistic satisfaction from its suffering."[8]

One can readily observe how Justine has become melancholic due to the loss (through neglect) of her parents. And one can see how this led her to search for a transformational object. The intrapsychic sadomasochistic activity is not apparent or observable in the character of Justine; it must be inferred by her psychopathology. In her mind, it isn't herself that Justine wants to destroy but the world. We must look to an earlier state of mind to discern the meaning of this. The child's omnipotent mind can destroy the world and make it disappear by magical thinking. The child pulls the blanket over her head and the world disappears (and the child cannot be seen). The world is herself, her ego; it is evil, and, when it is gone, Justine states: "No one will miss it." She means, "No one will miss *me* when I am gone because I am so bad." But it also carries a more narcissistically destructive message: "I will destroy the world because it has been such a disappointment to me."

Justine is sure there is life nowhere else in the universe. And because she alone guessed exactly how many beans there were in the jar at the wedding reception, one tends to believe what she says! "I know things; I've always known things," she tells Claire. There is no life like hers anywhere in the universe, she is unique and will destroy herself, everything and everyone in one grand gesture.

Viewing the ending of the film from the perspective of the inner world of the melancholic personality is horrifying. In this version of the story, Justine is *not* a helpful sister and aunt; she has brought disaster down on everyone. We see the playing out of narcissistic destruction to the point of suicide, not an unreasonable conclusion given the depth of depression and despair she felt. And how many times has she been there? How many times has Claire nursed her back from the brink of death? Maybe this time it really *is* the end. Did the end of the world happen literally, or was it all in her head?

Psyche

In 2040 a large asteroid will orbit close enough to Earth to be pulled by Earth's gravitational field. NASA scientists claim that the odds are remote that 2011 AG5 will make a direct impact, but those odds could change with future readings. Asteroids are really planetoids, space rocks that orbit the sun. There are millions of them, mostly small ones that would burn up in Earth's atmosphere. AG5 orbits the sun between Venus and Mars and is 460 feet wide. NASA's Near Earth Object Observations Program searches for and monitors threats to Earth from those asteroids large enough to do damage should they collide with Earth.

Apparently, sky anxiety is so pervasive that a NASA scientist, David Morrison, has coined the term "cosmophobia" to describe this new emotional and psychological disorder. Cosmophobia is the fear of the cosmos, particularly "the terror that the world will end by means of some astronomical occurrence."[9]

Jung was intensely preoccupied with UFOs (unidentified flying objects) in the late 1940s and 1950s when sightings were numerous. He gathered factual data and dream material that eventually became his book *Flying Saucers: A Modern Myth of Things Seen in the Skies* (1958). Jung considered UFOs to be either a mass hallucination or a factual occurrence. In his psychological exegesis of the UFO phenomena, Jung commented on the flying saucer as a symbol of wholeness constellated in the collective unconscious to compensate for the disintegrative and dissociative effect on the psyche caused by the cold war and the threat of a full-out nuclear war.

Wilfred Bion described catastrophic change as any change that threatens to subvert a given psychic order or structure, for better or for worse. Bion wrote: "It is catastrophic in the sense that it is accompanied by feelings of disaster in the participants [and that] it is sudden and violent in an almost physical way."[10] Resistance is always part of the change, but when resistance is predominant, the change becomes a catastrophe. Bion noted: "Mental evolution is catastrophic and timeless."[11] A feared inner truth deposes an established truth. Any significant movement in mental evolution challenges all our resistances and defenses.

Disasters close to home are monitored with alarm: climate change, rising sea levels, shrinking food supplies, increasing population, severe droughts, global financial instability, the collapse of governments, the collapse of the middle class, basic education moving out of reach, water supplies threatened, and more. One does not need to be entertained by a doomsday disaster movie; these days we seem to be living in one.

In *Archetype of the Apocalypse*, Edward Edinger described apocalyptic images as "the coming of the Self into conscious realization."[12] He believed the wheels of the apocalypse have long been set in motion. "It is a momentous event—literally world-shattering. This is what the content of the Apocalypse archetype presents: the shattering of the world as it has been, followed by its reconstitution."[13]

Edinger argued:

> The apocalyptic events depicted in the Book of Revelation are at hand. Jung's *Answer to Job*, if we can assimilate it, provides us with the meaning of these events. Certainly, Jung thought his understanding of these matters was worth his best efforts to communicate: "rather than allow laxity to let things drift toward the impending world catastrophe."[13]

Edinger's perspective is a continuation and extension of Jung's "myth of meaning." The process of individuation replaces the loss of containment in traditional religions or ideologies. Jung's psychology recognizes that the individual has a soul, that the ego is not the center of the personality, and that there is a regulating archetype within called the Self. In Jungian psychology there is a gradual change of the ego through repeated encounters with the shadow, anima/animus, and the Self. Contents of the unconscious reveal themselves to be inner contradictions to the ego's attitude and will. The ego learns it is not master in its own house. There are repeated, noisy collisions between the ego and the Self. "[God] is the name by which I designate all things which cross my willful path violently and recklessly."[14] This process leads to a gradual relativization of the ego and the establishment of a relationship between ego and Self. Jung believed in the cosmic and redemptive role of the human psyche. When we change ourselves, we change the world: "The world hangs on a thin thread, and that thread is the psyche of man."[15]

Meaning

Wolfgang Giegerich writes:

> Something new is trying to enter the consciousness of "modern man" in order to radically transform it. . . . Sinister and uncanny though it may be, meaninglessness is like a guest who knocks at our door asking for shelter. Perhaps we even need disillusionment through spiritual emptiness and meaninglessness as something necessary. . . . Perhaps the experience of meaninglessness is an initiation into the disillusioning and liberating knowledge that we are not ourselves divine children nor do we have to be, but mortal men: "children of death" born of the death of the child. And perhaps the loss of the center means a crumbling of the ontological totalitarianism of Christianity. Perhaps it could open up a distant vision of a psychology without ego and self, without wholeness and centroversion, without person and development, without meaning and salvation—a psychology devoid of all this theological ballast.[16]

For Giegerich, meaninglessness is meant to be something liberating, something that opens a door. It is not about learning to live without meaning but rather to experience how bondage to meaning can limit psychological evolution. Because we have taken Jung (and others) so seriously, we've overdone our "modern man in search of a soul," and we have outguessed and outrun "God's secret intentions."[17]

Meaninglessness is unbearable. It intrudes as an uninvited guest. The reaction is an attempt to plaster meaning onto events as a way of managing, tolerating, or controlling them. Jung questioned whether humans could survive without meaning. Jung's psychology was meant to address the alarm and anxiety of the modern individual and to replace lost meanings of religion and myth with a "myth of meaning." As part of this new myth, the human psyche has a cosmic role. The process of individuation assists in the evolution of the God-image. Jung writes in *Memories, Dreams, Reflections*: "That is the meaning of divine service, of the service which man can render to God, that light may emerge from the darkness, that the Creator may become conscious of His creation, and man conscious of himself."[18]

But if, as Giegerich suggests, meaninglessness may be a liberating guest, then the whole enterprise of meaning making is brought into question; it isn't thrown out altogether, but the potency of meaning is modified, lessened, attenuated. The rogue planet Melancholia, as the "uninvited guest," is an agent of catastrophic change and an image of the terror of change that we cannot understand and cannot influence. A menacingly huge planet swallows up a diminutive Earth. All biological development, all human evolution and culture, is destroyed. We feel small, helpless, and terrified.

At the beginning of the film, Justine lives in a state of longing. She does not fit into life. She cannot find meaning in life's rituals or ordinary human relationships. She knows that she cannot participate in such things because, for her, they are vacuous and empty.

According to Giegerich,

The longing for meaning is deluded about itself. . . . Meaning, where it indeed exists, is first of all an implicit fact of existence, it's a priori. It can never be the answer to a question; it is, conversely, an unquestioned and unquestionable certainty that predates any possible questioning. It is the groundedness of existence, a sense of embeddedness in life, of containment in the world—perhaps we could even say of in-ness as the logic of existence as such. Meaning exists if the meaning of life is as self-evident as the in-ness in water is for fish.

The search for meaning is in truth, but secretly, the longing for a state of "in-ness."[19]

Justine longs for what is not available. This is the dilemma for modern consciousness: we cannot go back, but how to go forward, and to what? Giegerich argues:

The kind of in-ness that is longed for, if it were indeed realized, would be intolerable for the modern subject. It would collide with our inalienable insistence on emancipated individuality and rationality. It would necessarily be felt as imprisonment, as a nightmare, of which the 20th century experience in totalitarian states and with fundamentalist sects has given us a taste.[20]

Understanding and feeling this dilemma induces a painful state of mind, feelings of loss, and disorientation. One searches for verisimilitude of "in-ness" (meaning) in a relationship, a psychology, or a theology. Instead, there is a collision between a previously held cluster of assumptions and a new, as yet unknown, reality.

Foreshadowing by an unusually bright star in the constellation Scorpio catches Justine's attention. Later, after she cannot get her horse Abraham to cross over the bridge, she looks up and sees that Melancholia has emerged into full view. She is compelled to understand what is happening and moves into the unknown. She walks into the woods at night, takes off her clothes, and lies near the water in the light of the planet. Justine now knows how to live with catastrophic change. Living with it would mean facing reality with full consciousness—no dissociation, no covering it over, or making it nicer than it is. Justine declares sharply, "You want to meet on the patio, sing a song, have a glass of wine? Why don't we meet on the toilet, Claire?" Justine tries to shake her sister out of her need for everything to be nice and wrapped up.

The soundtrack—Wagner's prelude to *Tristan und Isolde*—reflects the idea of catastrophic change. Wagner's prelude has been described by many musicologists as marking the start of the disintegration of Western tonal music. The so-called Tristan chord right at the beginning resolves in an unconventional manner for the times. Throughout the entire opera, the music never comes to a resolution until the very end when the lovers are dead. Instead, any momentary resolution in the music is merely a step to further chromatic dissonances. It is a musical representation of endless longing, yearning, desire, and delusional hopefulness.

We have Justine inside us as well as John, Claire, Leo, the parents, and the horses. John prefers to die rather than live through any significant change in his well-established life. He cannot tolerate a challenge or affront to his superior, know-it-all narcissism. Claire is overwrought with anxiety: "But where would Leo grow up?" She worries about the discontinuity caused by a huge shift. She clings to what is known. When John discovers the truth, he says, "There is nothing to do, there is no place to hide." The horses panic and behave frantically in response to the impending doom.

Tolerating living in a state of not knowing, without accepting an easy fix, is the doorway to a future psychology. *Melancholia* can be seen as a vision of catastrophe in which the idea of a saving myth or redemptive religion is lost, and the role of the individual psyche that Jung and Edinger put forward undergoes a shift. What we, as individuals, can do is limited. While not turning a blind eye and continuing to recognize the importance of doing whatever we can to help with the pressing issues of our time, there are hints that the effect of these efforts may be far less than we would hope.

How might Giegerich's "distant vision of a psychology without ego and self, without wholeness" appear? The end of the world as the end of ego gives a clue. It is not the loss of the ego but the loss of the ego in the position of the child, and it is the loss of the other since the child always has an other, something outside itself. The ego as the child has longings, fantasies, delusions, magical thinking, projections, and a belief in the totally other. The end of the world, as the end of the ego, is not just a relativization of the ego but the end of the ego as the centerpiece of psychology.

From Giegerich's perspective, it is a psychological act that Justine, as Soul, pulls the planet Melancholia from behind the sun and surrenders to it. She recognizes the other in Melancholia as belonging to herself, as her own interiority. The end of the world is the end of the other. The collision and swallowing up of Earth is the other finally coming home to itself. The dance of death that Melancholia does with Earth is the dance of negation, and it is the end of longing because there is no other to long for anymore.

In addition to terror of the future, and in part because of it, there exists collective melancholy. Blaming ourselves, in a melancholic way, results from an inflation that insists we should have and could have done better. We could and should have been better custodians of our planet, just as we could and should have been better parents to our children.

It is possible that we have lived to the end of what was once a useful system of moral life and is now an oppressive moralistic system that prevents life from opening, moving, and evolving. Our moralistic system is so much the water in which we live that we hardly realize it is there; we live it as an assumption. Every significant movement beyond our current way of thinking/feeling challenges our protective moralistic conditioning.

All our hopeful psychologies have a scent of moralism in one form or another. There is a correct way, a right way as opposed to the wrong way. There are writers who stimulate a sense of responsibility to the point of guilt toward what "we" have done and are doing to planet Earth. While these are facts not to be disputed, they appear to evoke an unhelpful response. One becomes drawn into a melancholic state of feeling bad, an emotional state that is a defense against further evolving, creative thinking, appropriate (not sentimental) feeling, and effective actions. All blaming and moralistic thinking can be viewed as a defense against the Kleinian depressive position, or against the "accomplished" stage of shadow integration.[21]

A quiet scene of the two moons late in the film foreshadows this authentic feeling state. One is Earth's moon, and the other is Melancholia shown in the nighttime sky as the moon's twin. The realization that Melancholia is in a direct collision course with Earth ushers in a period of quiet sadness. Justine is serious and calm. She eats, she is real, and she coaxes Claire into acceptance. The use of silence underscores the change, the shift; the two moons suggest a non-ego-centered event and are an image of the change in the cosmic syntax.

Greg Mogenson writes:

> The negation of the negation is more depressive and sad. Cringing at the thought of its former righteousness and naïveté, it [consciousness] starts to collapse from within and go under. Its shame, however, is a higher shame, the beginning of its sublation.[22]

End

Lars von Trier has powerfully expressed the current collective panic and anxiety about the end of the world. He searched for answers to the dilemmas of our time. By creating *Melancholia* he intuited a *telos* that is revealed in the film. The realization of this is far into the future, if at all: there are no more redemptive myths or a messianic *deus ex machina*. Instead, there exists a reality that we must face and manage with our limited human abilities. With the end of the other, there are no more victims and perpetrators, no more innocence and evil. There is no more tension or reconciliation of the opposites, no more "the one after the other [followed by] the side-by-side."[23] Instead, contradictions and opposites are squarely (logically) within each other and, perhaps most importantly, are *recognized and accepted as such*.

Melancholia is a ravishingly beautiful film with gorgeous images, breathtaking cinematography, and evocative music. Perhaps Lars von Trier did not have a visionary perspective as I have outlined in this essay, but he said that he hoped viewers would take a deeper look: "You can skate across the polished surface in this film. The style is polished, but underneath the smooth surface, there's content. And to get to that, you need to look beyond the polish."[24]

Notes

1 Nils Thorsen, "Melancholia Interview With Lars von Trier," *Made in Atlantis*, October 22, 2011.
2 Thorsen, "Interview."
3 Christopher Bollas, *The Shadow of the Object* (New York: Columbia University Press, 1987), 17.
4 Bollas, *Shadow*, 17.
5 Bollas, *Shadow*, 16–17.
6 Sigmund Freud, *Mourning and Melancholia, Vol 14, Standard Edition of the Complete Psychological Works of Sigmund Freud*, vol. 14 (London: Vintage, 2001), 251.
7 Freud, *SE* 14, 248.
8 Freud, *SE* 14, 251.
9 Ralfee Finn, "Tame Your Cosmophobia," *East Bay Express*, October 21, 2009.
10 Wilfred Bion, *"Transformations," Seven Servants* (New York: Jason Aronson, 1977), 8.
11 Wilfred Bion, *Attention and Interpretation* (London: Karnac, 1970), 108.
12 Edward F. Edinger, *Archetype of the Apocalypse: A Jungian Study of the Book of Revelation* (Chicago, IL: Open Court, 1999), 5.
13 Edinger, *Archetype*, 182.
14 Jung, *Letters*, 525.
15 William McGuire (ed.) and Richard F. C. Hull (trans.), *C. G. Jung Speaking: Interviews and Encounters* (Princeton: Princeton University Press, 1977), 303.
16 Wolfgang Giegerich, *Soul-Violence* (New Orleans: Spring Journal Books, 2008), 72.
17 From an unpublished letter by C. G. Jung quoted in Gerhard Adler, "Jung's Personality and Work," *Psychological Perspectives* (Spring 1975): 12. "Can man stand a further increase of consciousness? . . . Is it really worthwhile that man should progress morally and intellectually? . . . But I confess that I submitted to the divine power of this apparently insurmountable problem and I consciously and intentionally made my life miserable, because I wanted God to be alive and free from the suffering man has put upon him by loving his own reason more than God's secret intentions."

18 Jung, *MDR*, 338.
19 Wolfgang Giegerich, "The End of Meaning and the Birth of Man," *Journal of Jungian Theory and Practice* 6 (1) (2004): 2–5.
20 Giegerich, "End of Meaning," 3–4.
21 The concept of the depressive position was originally formulated by Melanie Klein in "A Contribution to the Psychogenesis of Manic-Depressive States" (1935). Klein observed that it follows an earlier stage in the development dominated by the presence of splitting wherein the good object is seen as separate from the bad object. The realization that the bad object and the good object are the same is accompanied by the "depressing" realization that hatred and aggression are directed toward the same object one loves. Klein and those after her wrote that the depressive position is never fully achieved, that it is worked on throughout one's life. Depressive position counters the natural tendency to split, to see matters in terms of mutually exclusive opposites.
    Regarding shadow integration, Wolfgang Giegerich writes, "The apprenticeship of consciousness is concluded. It has been a constant climb from complete innocence to full psychological awareness. . . . Now our logic can accept and affirm the inherent contradiction of our being, namely our *being* consciousness. . . . All the forms of killing of the previous stages—the theological, moralistic, enlightened, pietistic killings—have been overcome, not only empirically, but logically: because the form of otherness has been overcome." In "First Shadow, Then Anima, or the Advent of the Guest," in *Soul-Violence* (New Orleans: Spring Journal Books, 2008), 108.
22 Greg Mogenson, "Different Moments in Dialectical Movement," in *Dialectics and Analytical Psychology: The El Capitan Seminar* (New Orleans: Spring Journal Books, 2005), 94–5.
23 Jung, *CW 14*, para. 206.
24 Thorsen, "Interview."

Chapter 8

Body Ontology

The Blind Spot

For as long as I remember, I have had the following occurrence: a tiny blurry area appears in my visual field which then changes and looks like a piece of a jigsaw puzzle. This squiggly field follows and covers everything I look at and impairs my vision. It lasts about 20–30 minutes. The initial area of the visual distortion grows larger and larger until it dissipates at the edge of my visual field. I can use peripheral vision for some things but cannot read or do fine visual work. Years without an episode are followed by several episodes within a few months, mostly an annoyance. I discovered that they are called aura migraines, migraines that are not followed by an excruciating headache. They are apparently uncommon, although I have met people with similar symptoms. A few years ago, after one of those episodes, there was a period of 30 minutes during which I was dysphasic. I could not understand what I read, or what was spoken to me, nor could I make myself understood. Temporary dysphasia on occasion can follow such visual distortions. I was terrified by that first episode of dysphasia as I thought I might be having a stroke.

An aura migraine is caused by the dilation of blood vessels in my brain that affect the visual cortex. When I studied psychology, I wondered if an emotional reaction might trigger an episode or if the physical symptom was a replacement for having a conscious emotional reaction. I noticed that staring at a bright, glaring light will trigger an episode.

The Dropsical King and All His Majesty's Healers

> The conscious mind often knows little or nothing about its own transformation, and does not want to know anything. The more autocratic it is and the more convinced of the eternal validity of its truths, the more it identifies with them.[1]

Throughout college and into my early 30s, I was a classical musician, studying, playing, and teaching the violoncello. During a rehearsal for a church performance of *Elijah*, the oratorio by Mendelssohn, I noticed something strange happening with my left arm. It wasn't "working." I was missing notes and seemed unable to

DOI: 10.4324/9781003434009-9

play. Alarmed I quickly sought advice from an orthopedic physician, who upon examination and X-rays could find nothing wrong. The problem persisted.

That episode initiated a long saga of seeking advice and cures for a mysterious ailment. I went to numerous traditional doctors and alternative healers. I was diagnosed with bursitis in the shoulder and received injections, which gave me relief for a short period. I was diagnosed with rheumatoid arthritis, juvenile rheumatoid arthritis, and Still's disease but nothing really fit as I had no other symptoms. Then I had occasional rashes and fevers and was tentatively diagnosed with Lupus, but the tests did not confirm it. I changed my diet and changed my cello coach. My anxiety increased, which made it worse. I was able to play in a limited way and to continue teaching my many students, but anything more was out of the question. I was desperate, miserable, and depressed.

I wrote down my dreams and noted that many of them had to do with my actual cello, my instrument. My Jungian analyst and I examined each one carefully for clues to understand my predicament. The dreams were as mysterious as my ailment. There was no easy message to extract. The dreams became more perplexing. Yet I felt sure there was a key in them to unlock the mystery of what was happening to me.

I was desperate to find a cure. I continued to consult with numerous doctors and healers. I tried traditional cures and alternative cures, acupuncture, and the Alexander technique. Nothing worked, and without fully understanding what was happening to me, eventually I gave up music as my main career focus. I began graduate school in clinical psychology and subsequently became a psychologist and eventually a Jungian analyst.

> Pitilessly it is seen from another planet that the king is growing old, even before he sees it himself: ruling ideas, the "dominants," change, and the change, undetected by consciousness, is mirrored only in dreams.[2]

During my studies to become an analyst, I read Jung's Collected Works, volume 14, *Mysterium Coniunctionis*.[3] Chapter IV, *Rex and Regina*, contains many alchemical stories on the theme of the renewal of the king. Some are simple while others are long and convoluted. Jung described the symbolism of the king as the ruling dominant of consciousness, the organizing principle of central value, the Self. In alchemy, the image of the king was closely associated with gold, the king of metals and the one of highest value. In early societies, it was believed that having an ailing or old king was not good for the health of the society. To ensure a healthier one, the king might be killed or replaced by a younger, more vigorous one. There are numerous variations on this theme. At the beginning of a fairytale, there may be a problem in the kingdom such as an old or sick king, a missing queen, a king who is unable to produce an heir, or any problem that impairs the health of the kingdom.

In *Mysterium*, Jung describes an amusing story of a certain king who, as he is about to go to battle, asks for "special" water. He then drinks so much that "all his limbs were filled and all his veins inflated, and he himself becomes discolored."[4] He calls upon all the physicians in his realm to come and heal him. The Egyptian physicians try first and subject the king's body to various procedures. They tear him to pieces, grind him to powder, and then mix the powder with medicines before putting him into a heated chamber. When he is brought out, he appears dead, but the physicians then wash him and subject him to further procedures. However, nothing works to restore him.

Angry at their failure, the king then calls upon the Alexandrian physicians, who repeat similar procedures but in addition mix the corpse with a *sal ammoniac*, Alexandrian *nitre*, and linseed oil. There is more heating and waiting, and, finally, by all these procedures, the king is cured and restored to his full potency.

In the margins of my copy of *Mysterium Coniunctionis*, as I studied the text, I noted all the procedures that were applied to the king: sweating, grinding, mixing, heating, washing, drying, and tearing apart, to name a few. I compared them to images from the dreams I had about my cello during those terrible years. What a comparison! Just as the king, as a ruling principle of consciousness, is the *prima materia* that undergoes many "questionable" procedures for renewal, my cello as the *prima materia* in my dreams went through various "questionable" procedures. It struck me that a renewal process had been at hand, quite beyond my ego awareness.

Playing music was of utmost importance to me, and I could not imagine my life without music at its center. My life energy was bound up with playing the cello, and because I was identified with the cello, I suffered the "torments" that my cello endured in my dreams. Furthermore, I was resistant to change as I could not imagine what the change might be.

What follows are the dreams I had over that period of about three years during which I suffered from anxiety, helplessness, depression, and uncertainty about my mysterious physical condition. They are as they were written at that time in my dream journal. Of course, there were many other dreams, but these are the dreams that had the image of my cello. I include two dreams with the image of the king, as that is an unusual dream image.

I'm in a castle. There is a room where the dead old king is. It is bolted and shut and they leave him there for many years. Someone is showing it to me when we hear noises inside. The door is opened and what we see is that someone has ransacked the place and made off with the king's body! All that is left is the chair where the King was sitting.

I'm walking with a musician friend to my studio. I tell him to wait so I can show him my cello. I go into the studio. On the floor is a broken endpin. Then I see a cello chipped in the side and broken at the neck. I think maybe this is not my cello, that there had been another one there. Then I see my cello case open and another cello is lying there also broken at the neck and chipped on the sides and full of cracks. I am horrified and upset beyond words, so much so that I can't even cry or say anything. I go running outside. Then my friend is holding the two broken cellos which now look like flat circular discs. I try to cry.

I am playing my cello and when I show it to someone, I notice that the left side is sunk down, depressed, and this is the first time I had noticed it.

I am practicing my cello. The bridge has collapsed between the A and G strings so that the levels of the strings are different, and it is now difficult to play.

I am at a cello lesson when the lower left back part of my cello falls off revealing blackish-gray worms that are living inside. They are eating the wood and making cocoons that are white. They are eating the bridge and all around it.

My cello had gotten wet somehow and lost its shape, and the edges are unglued, especially the bottom front is loose.

I'm playing my cello in an orchestra. There are too many strings on it. There are eight strings and I want to go back to having just 4. It is confusing to play.

I'm rehearsing a Brahms sextet. A green worm comes out of my left side. I am embarrassed about it. Then I feel another worm moving in my left hand and around my wrist. I don't know how or if it will come out, but it is very disconcerting to feel it moving. My god, I am infested with worms!

I take my cello into the shower with me. It needs to be cleaned and humidified periodically. I think a lot of water is getting inside, but when I take it out, it is dry inside. I've locked the door because there is a man outside who would be horrified by what I am doing and wouldn't let me clean it like that!

I am someplace with my cello. There is something wrong with it. Someone notices smoke coming out of it and I look inside and sure enough, there is a fire inside the cello! I quickly go and splash water inside to put the fire out. It will need repairs!

I see the wood on my cello is becoming weird like it has advanced dry rot, a fungus. I pull off a section that reveals numerous orange eggs. I take the cello to a woman repair person who agrees to fix it.

A new girl student comes for her lesson, and I tune her cello. The cello has a special device in the peg box which when the strings are tuned perfectly a square is formed. The strings are connected to each other through this device and if one string is not in tune, the whole device is not a perfect square.

I have a date with the king. He wants to take me to dinner. I'm not thinking much about it. Then when he comes to the house it turns out to be the son of the king, the young king. I am surprised. I knew the old king was interested, but I was blasé about that. He is the son who is in the middle of his prime.

When I had all those dreams, I was unaware of the extensive symbolism of the renewal of the king, except as I had encountered it in myths and fairytales. The alchemical procedures to renew the king were completely unknown to me. Jung wrote,

> the conscious mind is a bad judge of its own situation and often persists in the illusion that its attitude is just the right one and is only prevented from working because of some external annoyance. If the dreams were observed it would soon become clear why the conscious assumptions have become unworkable. And if, finally, neurotic symptoms appear, then the attitude of consciousness, its ruling idea, is contradicted, and in the unconscious there is a stirring up of those archetypes that were the most suppressed by the conscious attitude.[5]

That series of dreams makes for an impressive presentation wherein my cello is undergoing alchemical procedures of breakdown and transformation. Those dreams presented shocking images as if the unconscious were attempting to get the attention of consciousness. The dreams also portray simply what was happening to me psychically that I couldn't think about. In either case, the projection of importance on my cello was falling away, as I was outgrowing my music career. I was a "sleeping beauty" in thralldom to music and my cello. A few years after those dreams, I had another dream in which the "house of music" was burning down. Inside were all my musical instruments, my sheet music, accessories, and my beloved cello. I was running to see if I could try, at least, to salvage my cello.

It is tempting to think that I was being directed by "something mysterious" in my psyche. But what happened to me wasn't mysterious at all. In many ways my satisfaction with my career in music had been waning, despite my clinging to it, and my denials. The petty competition among musicians was wearisome as well as the paucity of well-paying work close to where I lived. But I couldn't find a way to leave it. I don't think I wanted to think about it! My mysterious ailment was a hysterical symptom, a "neurotic symptom," an expression of something I was not able to be aware of at the time. It was the blockage from which I could not move on nor go back. My symptoms were present at times, then disappeared, and then were back again. I clung to music and my cello in desperation, like being on an island with no other visible land.

Having been in Jungian psychotherapy and around the local Jung group in Los Angeles since I was a student at UCLA, I suspect I had a feeling for wanting to be an analyst that I kept away from and out of my mind, not allowing myself to have the thought about something that felt completely unattainable. Those Jungian analysts were folks, mostly men, with MDs and PhDs! Such an accomplishment was far out of reach for me. However, in addition to achieving my BA with honors from UCLA in music, I minored in psychology, taking all the required courses I would need should I ever think of applying to psychology graduate school. Still, the idea of pursuing psychology was far from my mind as I suffered those years of not being able to play my beloved cello.

During my years of graduate school and internships, I had a busy schedule of cello students, organizing student recitals, and I continued to play chamber music with friends. Free from the pressure of playing as a career, my symptoms gradually disappeared.

> the aging of a psychic dominant is apparent from the fact that it expresses the psychic totality in ever-diminishing degree. One can also say that the psyche no longer feels wholly contained in the dominant, whereupon the dominant loses its fascination and no longer grips the psyche so completely as before. On the other hand its content and meaning are no longer properly understood, or what is understood fails to touch the heart.[6]

I had been asleep to a deeper, fuller psychic reality, living my feeling values through music. That might have been enough, but I had encountered Jungian analysis which planted the thought of *being* a Jungian analyst. The syntax of my life changed, as if from Baroque to Classical music. Both forms are legitimate, but being a Jungian analyst was more suitable for me. The "mysterious illness" became something of a "vanishing mediator,"[7] a term to describe something that bridges two positions and then disappears when no longer needed, that is, when the change of syntax is complete.

Taking My Lumps

A decade after I became a Jungian analyst, I was diagnosed with a low-grade lymphoma after I discovered first one then two marble-sized lumps in my upper left neck. I was biopsied and scanned, and although only two cancerous lymph nodes were found, this type of lymphoma is slow growing and incurable. I received radiation treatment to shrink those nodes, and the lymphoma went into remission. As well as spreading throughout my lymphatic system, with each year, there is an increased chance of it transforming into a more aggressive form of lymphoma that would require aggressive chemotherapy. I was advised to live my life sooner rather than later, as my future was uncertain and unpredictable.

I was turbocharged by the diagnosis. At first, I worked to mentally adjust to this new set of conditions. I read many books about cancer, living, and dying, and I explored alternative treatments. If I had ten years to live, how should I spend them? I traveled to Europe, India, Brazil, and Turkey. I wrote papers, delivered talks, and became more involved with everything. Whatever drew me, I went to it. I put my condition into an alchemical vessel with the question, What is this about? I recognized that my lymphoma could be random but what if my psychology had something to do with it? My condition was unknown to anyone, except for a closest few, for over seven years.

There is an abundance of material written about the relationship between mind, emotions, body symptoms, illness, disease, and pain. Psychogenic or "magical" causes of disease and illness have always existed. Witches or bad spells were thought to make someone ill or cause death. The moralistic attitude toward some kinds of illness persists to this day, especially about cancer. "It is individuation that is not being consciously lived, so it grows in the body" is one part of the dogma I heard in Jungian circles. If one doesn't feel certain emotions, they turn into symptoms, in psychoanalytic circles. There is some kind of blaming, a moralistic viewpoint that amounts to "If you get sick, you are doing something wrong. You are missing something." The opposite view claims that illness or any disease of the body has absolutely nothing to do with the mind or emotions. Abnormal cell mutations cause cancer. Eventually, we all die of something, even if old age. No amount of psychological scrutiny or "individuation" can cure that.

I delved into all that literature in psychoanalysis and in Jung's writings. I searched through all the *Collected Works* and his *Letters* for anything about illness, cancer, and the psyche. No reference escaped my scrutiny. I found a useful comment in a letter from Jung to Joachim Knopp in 1946.

One can say that it is advisable to approach every illness from the psychological side as well, because this may be extraordinarily important for the healing process. When these two aspects work together, it may easily happen that the cure takes place in the intermediate realm, in other words that it consists of a *complexio oppositorum*, like the *lapis*. In this case the illness is in the fullest sense a stage of the individuation process.[8]

Twelve years after my first treatment, another lump appeared snuggled deep in my left armpit. Barely palpable at first, it had that unmistakable hard, lumpy feel like the first ones in my neck. Biopsy and scans later, it turned out to be a single node that was slowly growing. When it became the size of a golf ball, it was treated with a newer form of radiation. The node quickly shrunk and disappeared.

Visits to my oncologist gradually went from every three months to every six, to once per year to, every so often, to . . . well, to whenever I felt I should check in, mostly, to see if my very likable oncologist was *himself* still alive. "Why am I not dead?" I once asked him. "You apparently have a slow form of lymphoma, one that doesn't transform." In the beginning, my mantra was, "If I can transform, then the lymphoma doesn't have to." This was perhaps a "magical thinking" perspective but nevertheless an exceedingly helpful one at the time.

I was familiar with Jung's writing on the necessity of "impossible problems"[9] that force development in an individual and his suggestion that a higher level of consciousness is generally available. He wrote,

all the greatest and most important problems of life are fundamentally insoluble. . . . They can never be solved, but only outgrown. . . . Everyone must possess that higher level, at least in embryonic form, and must under favorable circumstances be able to develop this potentiality.[10]

Of course, I wondered whether one can apply this to a physical illness such as lymphoma. I would put it in an alchemical vessel as I do with an emotion, a dream, or a fantasy.

When I encountered the works of Wolfgang Giegerich, I came across this illuminating quote:

Even psychogenic body symptoms and affects are at bottom thoughts, but, as it were, "materialized" thoughts, thoughts submerged, sunk into the natural, physical medium of body or emotion.[11]

And a fuller statement on this matter:

And a psychology informed by Alchemy would have the task of freeing "the spirit Mercurius," i.e., the thought that is imprisoned in "the matter" (in the image, the emotion, the body symptom) imprisoned in the Real. In general, we could establish the following series: body symptom is submerged emotion,

emotion is submerged image, image is submerged thought, and conversely, thought is sublated image, image is sublated emotion, emotion is sublated body reaction or behavior.[12]

This approach added to my considerations of body symptoms and illness. Besides emotions and feeling, there is thinking. Not the ordinary definition of thinking but rather, thinking as "the art to allow the matter that we are dealing with to speak for itself."[13] The ego doesn't *do* it but rather allows the autonomous psyche to speak.

The soul dimension, as Giegerich describes it, is not some mystical or a numinous psychological place; however, access to it requires a movement that leaves behind an ego-bound, emotional, and personalistic perspective. The movement happens and allows one to be in a different status of consciousness. Thinking, as Giegerich utilizes it, is not about the so-called thinking function of Jung's ego typology, not an intellectual activity, or any natural activity of the psyche. It is a *contra naturam*, against nature. There are no moralistic or developmental ideas attached to the idea of thought being submerged in the body symptom. It is an alchemical notion that speaks of freeing Mercurius, the spirit, from matter. In such cases, one must allow oneself to become a sublated moment of the matter at hand. I allow myself to be reached by the soul as much as the soul reaches me. Freeing Mercurius is freeing the living dialectical process that is the soul, the Self, the autonomous psyche.

A few years ago, I had a full body scan, and there was no sign of lymphoma. Last year my oncologist retired. A remnant of superstition makes me hesitant to write that perhaps my lymphoma has been "thought through." The "submerged thought" was sublated to emotion, to image, and then to thought. All the years that I have worked with it, one way or another, have brought about a sublation of lymphoma from physical symptom to thought. In the first chapter of this book, I described the movement from the physical manifestation of lymphoma to emotions. During the many years of work with my "new analyst," I became aware of and fluent in emotions, the bearable, the unbearable, the contradictory, the refractory, the unacceptable, and the overwhelming. However, it seems something remained happily submerged in emotions.

There have been reports of spontaneous remission in some types of lymphoma, where it comes and goes and then disappears. On the other hand, my lymphoma is overdue for another appearance. The notion that it is "submerged thought" sounds ludicrous to the scientific medical model. But this idea interests me just because it turns scientific thought on its head. It reminds me of what has been discarded in contemporary thinking, that humans have a body *and* a soul and there is something more than the cells that make up what we are. It affirms alchemical ideas, the *contra naturam*, and their relevance to psychology today.

In *The Soul's Logical Life*, Giegerich writes that alchemy was an engine that worked off one status of consciousness to another, that the alchemists intuited the new status and used the best language they had available, imagistic thinking, to describe the new status.[14] Alchemical processes still happen today to bring about transformations and movement to a new level of consciousness.

Much of what has happened to me might be attributed to psychological development and the aging process; however, living with the constant possibility of serious illness and death proved beneficial to me. I was always "up against the wall." I often felt like Dmitri Shostakovich composing music in the era of Stalin.[15]

I ask the question, what is the thought submerged in my symptoms or condition be it scotoma, lymphoma, or the mysterious condition that pushed me from music into psychology? The latter was "a vanishing mediator," a concept which mediates the transition between two opposed concepts and thereafter disappears."[16] It is a process by which the dialectic of negation, and the negation of that negation, is a sublation to a new level of consciousness. The old level is negated, taken apart, but preserved and brought to a new level. Being a Jungian analyst is playing music within a different syntax. Being a Jungian analyst *now* compared to being a Jungian analyst 30 years ago is playing music within yet a different syntax, perhaps like the shift from Romantic to Modern music. As I described elsewhere,[17] modern music attempts to eschew the hegemony of tonality, a basic component of the syntax of music for the past hundreds of years. Composing in the 20th and 21st centuries is analogous to living without religion or God. "I don't believe in him, but I miss him," wrote Julian Barnes.[18] Composing in the modern era has the echo of tonality always in the background. Being a Jungian analyst today is in the shadow of earlier religiosity and the unquestioned idealism of Jung.

The illnesses I have written about have received the longest and most attention, but there have been others. A nasty case of shingles of the trigeminal nerve that was not diagnosed until I was outside the window for the traditional medical protocol, heavy doses of the antiviral Valtrex. The pain in my ear, my teeth, and my face became so intense that I ended up one night in the ER where a neurologist was able to give me appropriate IV medications for nausea, pain, and inflammation of the nerve. Something brittle cracked in me when I recovered, thankfully with little to no post-herpetic neuralgia, as many others have. Personally, a layer of brittle narcissism, a protective shell cracked. I knew when it happened, I could feel it, and I could think it. That shift could happen only through the brutal assault of shingles. "I am not what I think I am" became a living, felt reality. When I have allowed these assaults to happen, to engage with them, I have been irrevocably altered.

"Thinking" the symptom, allowing the thought to speak for itself, is for me the most significant approach to physical symptoms and illness. Not thinking in the sense of an intellectual exercise or an ego activity and not thinking as one of Jung's typologies. It is allowing the symptom to speak for itself, allowing the matter to have a voice. This approach doesn't make sense to the perspective that puts ego concerns first. It can sound moralistic as if that is what one must do to cure oneself. But there is no cure in this perspective. I didn't cure my lymphoma. I don't know that it isn't there lurking in my body, undetectable, waiting for its next cue to enter, stage left. I can think with Jung that perhaps the lymphoma was outgrown, or with Giegerich that the spirit Mercurius submerged in those lumpy lymph nodes and has been freed. I can also take the criticism that I have wrapped meaning around these difficult experiences. Yes, I have. I do make "meaning" out of everything significant that happens, risking perhaps seeing significance where there is none. However, I sometimes quip that compared to 30 years ago, I am a sober Jungian.

Scotomata

I wonder about the thought submerged in this lifelong symptom of scintillating aura migraine. It creates a blind spot, a temporary scotoma. I can't see, and on occasion, I can't process verbally. The natural process of seeing is negated so the blind spot makes possible a different way of seeing. Temporarily I am abducted from the ordinary world and taken to the underworld. When it happens, the best thing to do is to hide out in a dark room and sleep for a while. I had one just the other day. It's crazy. Being abducted is a mythological way to describe the egoic realm being disrupted by the soul dimension. Persephone is grabbed by Hades, and innocence is negated and initiated into "that other" reality.

I think of how well things must work to keep the body parts working together and humming along, and how the slightest disruption in a biochemical, a hormone, a ligament, a blood vessel, or one of the myriad body parts can set the whole in a downward spiral. The aura migraine physical symptom has not gone away. It shows up suddenly, unexpectedly, "out of the blue." I think of it as *ille fugax Mercurius*, that shy, fleeting, fleeing, evasive, disruptive Mercurius, a thing that is not a thing, that which negates the visible and is a constant reminder of what is *not* there is *truly there*, and vice versa. That devil Mercurius has plagued me, created such troubles, brought such riches.

Notes

1   Carl G. Jung, CW 14, *Mysterium Coniunctionis: An Inquiry into the Separation and Synthesis of Psychic Opposites in Alchemy*, 2d ed., Bollingen Series 20 (Princeton, NJ: Princeton University Press, 1970), para. 503.
2   Jung, CW 14, para. 504.
3   Jung, CW 14.
4   Jung. CW 14, para. 357.
5   Jung, CW 14, para. 505.
6   Jung, CW 14, para. 505.
7   Tony Myers, *Slavoj Zizek* (Abingdon, UK: Routledge, 2003). Term introduced by Fredric Jameson in an essay on Max Weber, later used in psychoanalysis and by Slavoj Zizek.
8   Jung, *Letters*, Bollingen Series, 95: 1–2 (Princeton, NJ: Princeton University Press, 1973), 429.
9   Carl G. Jung and Claire Douglas, *Visions: Notes of the Seminar Given in 1930–1934 by C.G. Jung*, Bollingen Series 99 (Princeton, NJ: Princeton University Press, 1997), 320.
10 Jung, *Alchemical Studies*, CW 13, para. 18.
11 Wolfgang Giegerich, *The Soul Always Thinks*, vol. 4, Collected English Papers (New Orleans: Spring Journal Books, 2010), 334.
12 Giegerich, *Soul Always Thinks*, CEP 4, 334.
13 Giegerich, *Soul Always Thinks*, CEP 4, 16.
14 Wolfgang Giegerich, *The Soul's Logical Life: Towards a Rigorous Notion of Psychology* (Frankfurt am Main: Peter Lang, 1998), 134 ff.

15 See this book, Chapter 6.
16 Myers, *Slavoj Zizek*, 38.
17 Pamela J. Power, "How Does Music Think?," Forthcoming in *Essays on 'The Soul's Logical Life' in the Work of Wolfgang Giegerich*. Jennifer M. Sandoval, Colleen El-Bejjani, and Pamela J. Power (Eds.) (Abingdon, UK: Routledge, 2023).
18 Julian Barnes, *Nothing to Be Frightened Of* (New York: Alfred A. Knopf, 2008), 1.

Chapter 9

The "Arcane Substance" in the World of Gaming

In June 2020, I read a review of a video game that had just been released, called *The Last of Us Part II*.[1] Previously, I never noticed or paid attention to video game reviews. But this one was long and prominent in the *Sunday New York Times*[2] and something in that review caught my attention. The two reviewers were seasoned "gamers." They wrote of being stirred by the game, by the beauty of the graphics, and they described how the player is confronted with moral choices that are emotionally challenging and deeply affecting. I subsequently read other reviews that described this game and other video games *as art*.

A video game as Art? Emotionally affecting? What was going on? The last video game I played was *Tetris* in the 1980s. These and other articles stirred in my mind for several months until early in 2022 my curiosity led me to find out, firsthand, what was going on in the world of gaming. I bought a refurbished Play Station 4, and a copy of *The Last of Us Part II*, the game that grabbed my interest by that *New York Times* article.

My attempt to play was a disaster. The graphics were gorgeous, but I struggled to use the controller and make my character move around. I deduced that I must be going about this the wrong way. I bought *The Last of Us Part I*,[3] the precursor that was released in 2013 and recently remastered for the PS4. Surely, this would be an easier place to begin. But it was no better, and I was no better. I could not get my character to walk across the room, open the door, or do any activities that were required of me, the player. Later difficulties, such as escaping from the dangerous "infected people," seemed entirely out of reach.

During that time, in frustration, I texted a friend who had played video games for years and told her of my plight. She responded by telling me that when she first began to play *World of Warcraft*, she spent an entire day learning to get her character (avatar) to turn around. Armed with her reassurance, I persevered with the controller and educated myself with YouTube videos. I experimented with other games, easier ones to hone my skills, thinking I would return to *The Last of Us*, down the road. Then in July of 2022, in the *Los Angeles Times*, I noticed a review of a new video game called *Stray*,[4] a game where one plays as an orange tabby cat that meows and jumps around in an underground city, seeking to find the lost outside world.[5] It sounded delightful so I quickly downloaded *Stray* onto my PS4.

DOI: 10.4324/9781003434009-10

I still wasn't very good, but the game was easier, and I found it compelling to learn how to outrun the deadly Zurks, evade the Sentinels, and make it up to the control room to open the city. A skilled player can get through the game in under two hours. It took me more than 12 hours (spread out over weeks) to finish the game. It was a triumph for me to persevere during parts where I was killed and eaten by the Zurks and zapped by the Sentinels. I joined a Facebook group devoted to the game *Stray* and received help and encouragement from members around the world. One especially helpful suggestion came early from a young man in India who told me to make Stray run fast, zigzag back and forth, and simply outrun the Zurks. Later, in return, I gave suggestions to players new to the game. "Practice running that part several times before you push the lever that sets the Zurks upon you!" I was happy and sad when I finished the game. My Facebook friends felt the same. Will there be a *Stray*, part 2?

Both *Stray* and *The Last of Us* are single-player games set in post-apocalyptic worlds. In *Stray*, the goal is to open the city that has been sealed over by a huge dome for hundreds of years. There had been an unnamed pandemic, and all humans had perished. It now was infested by mutant Zurks and inhabited by human-like robots, who timelessly carry on the routine tasks they were made to do hundreds of years earlier by their human overlords. In *The Last of Us Part I*, the world has been ravaged by a pandemic, caused by the fungus cordyceps. Large numbers of the population succumbed or were killed in attempts to control the spread of the fungus.

In *The Last of Us Part I*, the goal is to make a vaccine against the fungal infection whereas in *Stray*, the goal is simply to open the city. *Stray* is a straightforward game, a story with a poignant but happy ending. *The Last of Us Part I* is different. I had read about the game and knew what happens at the end and the controversies the ending generated. I was thrown into deep curiosity by the ending as well as the idea of a vaccine as the "arcane substance" from alchemy. Finally, there remained something perplexingly different about the two games.

Stray

Stray begins with four cat friends living in an idyllic nature setting, playing and sleeping together until Stray, an orange tabby falls into a deep abyss and lands in a desolate, dark underground area full of detritus. He finds his way into a "dead city" and while making his way through it, he encounters a helpful friend B12, a small robotic drone, which rides in a backpack made to fit "a small quadruped." B12 can read signs, decipher codes, and otherwise be an advisor. B12 turns out to be a downloaded but corrupted consciousness of a dead human scientist.

There are Zurks, one-eyed creatures that evolved from mutated bacteria that were designed by now long-dead humans to consume garbage. They are disgusting creatures that go after anything living, including a small orange tabby cat. Stray must outrun the Zurks when they attack, and later elude the Sentinels, roving robotic devices that scan for any sign of life, and upon discovery, shoot it down.

Stray outruns the Zurks, escapes the scanning Sentinels, and with help from B12, achieves the goal of reaching the control room. A large dome opens and natural sunlight streams into the city, which eradicates the remaining Zurks and renders the Sentinels powerless. *Stray* then leaves the city and returns to the idyllic nature of his home shown at the beginning of the game. But after all that Stray has been through and achieved, he is not the same cat. He looks the same, he acts the same, but he is a "sublated" cat, I joked to myself. Sublation is originally a philosophical term that means negated, changed, preserved, and raised up to another level, all those things at once. *Stray* is no longer an innocent cat, but one that has incorporated all the experiences he had gone through. He is a "cat that is not a cat," like a "stone that is not a stone," a philosophical cat rather than an ordinary cat. All the challenges taken on have suffused the cat with another level of consciousness. There is absolutely no evidence for my fanciful interpretation in the actual game!

The Last of Us Part I

In *The Last of Us Part I*, the goal is to find a cure, a vaccine that will protect against the fungal infection that turns one into a zombie-like creature that only lives to infect others. An obnoxious, foul-mouthed teenage girl, Ellie, is discovered to be immune to the fungus after she had become infected. The reason for this is unknown. A group of doctors wants to make a vaccine from her blood. She becomes cargo to be transported from Boston to Salt Lake City. It is a tricky task because the "authorities" have developed a scanner. Ellie is not ill but tests positive with the scanner and if caught would be killed on the spot. A deal is made with a hardened smuggler, Joel, to secretly transport her to the group of doctors out west.

The challenge of learning to play a video game was strangely compelling. It appealed to my gadget-loving side. But the idea of the *arcane substance* caught the attention of the Jungian analyst in me. When the ending of Part I created heated discussions among gamers and in online forums, this only added to my curiosity about the *arcane substance*.

The Arcane Substance

The "arcane substance" is a term that has many meanings and many names: *aqua vitae*, *lapis philosophorum*, and Mercurius, an elusive energy. "Arcane" means secret, mysterious, obscure, or enigmatic. It means something we don't understand. The alchemists didn't understand the substances they encountered and worked with. In trying to make gold, they searched for a special transforming substance or spirit that would turn base metals into gold. But the gold they were seeking wasn't ordinary gold but philosophical gold. The lapis, the stone, a term for the goal, was described in paradoxical, enigmatic terms as vile, cheap, and not worth anything yet also most perfect and precious. It is everywhere yet invisible and nowhere to be found—solid, yet liquid, etc. The beginning is the goal. It takes gold to make gold. The *prima materia* and the *lapis* are one. The arcane substance is the *prima materia*, the transformative agent, and the gold, that is, the goal, itself. The "arcane substance" is what moves, that is, transforms to a higher logical status, a higher status of consciousness.

In searching to understand the phenomena of matter, the alchemists used paradoxes to describe what they discovered. A paradox can encompass the contradictory natures of one entity. But a paradox is a stopgap on the way to a fuller understanding. It is a useful placeholder until a future understanding is revealed. Once the wave-particle paradox described the different ways that light behaved until the discovery of quantum mechanics more adequately explained the phenomenon.

For many, getting the COVID vaccine became a much-sought "arcane substance," a preventative from serious illness or death. I sat in the four-hour car wait at Dodger Stadium in Los Angeles to get one of the first COVID vaccines, while my spouse, who accompanied me, refused the new-fangled vaccine and opted for "wait and see" and perhaps a more traditionally made vaccine. For many years, vitamin D was a literal arcane substance for me. My blood serum level remained stubbornly below normal, and I was told to get it higher. I tried unsuccessfully for years until with research and experimentation, I discovered how to raise it. Then I was told, hey watch out, don't let the level get too high. This is the poison and panacea idea that is built into nearly all our medicines today: too much can make it toxic while too little renders it ineffective. But it is not a *true* paradox because we understand how most medicines work.

The alchemists believed that the "arcane substance" was always present but not recognized as such. Invisible, but visible, the alchemists said. There are old alchemical pictures of people going about their daily business unaware of what was all around them—the precious, most valuable substance.

I thought about *The Last of Us* as a dream and when working with dreams, one turns things upside down or inside out to allow the dream to reveal its meaning. What is chasing us is something that is coming to change us. It is the *coniunctio* (the coming together of the old and the new, conscious and unconscious aspects) at hand, but not yet recognized. We are afraid of what seems scary to us, what seems threatening, even deadly threatening. We don't want to die in our dreams because naturally we are identified with the dream ego that wants to survive as is. Dying in dreams means a change so big that the ego perspective dies into a different consciousness.

In this light, rather than finding a cure, an "arcane substance," *against* the deadly cordyceps fungus, one can think of the cordyceps fungus as itself the "arcane substance." It is there to radically transform humanity and take it to another level. From the perspective of the people in the game and as the player of the game, cordyceps is viewed *only* as deadly and threatening. But viewed as a powerful transforming agent, its intent is to break down current collective consciousness (ways of thinking and feeling) for a new consciousness to emerge. That's what fungi do. They break down what is already dying. "They decompose dead and dying organisms and move nutrients back into the cycle of life," as shown in the documentary film, *Fantastic Fungi*.[6] It is an agent of sublation, to negate, preserve, and raise to another level.

The two main characters in *The Last of Us Part I*, Joel and Ellie, at first are repelled by each other. He is a crusty, hardened smuggler, she is a bratty teenager. The job of transporting her forces them to work together, and they become agents of change for each other and themselves. Ellie was infected by the fungus but developed an immunity that shows on her arm as scars. They hope to make a vaccine from her, but in a way, she already is a proto-version of a vaccine. She has taken on the deadly element which has become incorporated into her body, so she is a new kind of human. If we think that the true "arcane substance" is the cordyceps fungus itself, it is both the disease and cure of itself, the paradox of poison/panacea. But the cure is not for the individual human person, but for the larger human collective consciousness. At the end of Part I, Joel discovers that the doctors will not simply take her blood to make a cure, but they will use her brain. As Ellie is prepared for surgery, Joel saves her from certain death. Ellie had been prepared to sacrifice herself for the possibility of saving humanity, but Joel was having none of that. After rescuing Ellie, he lies and tells her that there are others who are immune to the fungus (there are not) and that Ellie doesn't need to be cut open and sacrifice herself. On discussion forums about the game, the argument was, and still is, whether Joel was selfish not to allow the possibility of a vaccine to be made from Ellie's brain. Because he had come to love her as a replacement for his lost daughter, he would not give her up. He sacrificed humanity, the implication of Joel's decision at the end of the game.

Violence

When I first began to play *The Last of Us*, I gradually became adept at using my gun, shooting from a distance, aiming carefully so that I only used one shot to kill whatever the enemy was in that section. However, I soon discovered that I ran out of ammunition. In many cases, the only way to get past a section was to sneak up on a person and do a "stealth kill," which involves grabbing ahold of the person and killing him—or her—with one's bare hands. I was at first repulsed by this activity and preferred to do the killing from a distance, with a gun. But there is not enough ammo lying around and the most efficient and safe way is to sneak up and pick the enemy off one by one. One is forced to feel the violence in one's body through the haptics of the controller. I had to learn to tolerate the intimacy of death and killing, as well as being killed, which happened many times. I had not anticipated this aspect of the game. Nor did I anticipate that the early kills would give way to the necessity of killing the more lethal forms of the infected by using more lethal methods. The "clickers" required a "shiv" that you shove into the neck. It creates a bloody mess! But it is a necessity to get past them to the next part of the game.

There is a long-lived dispute about violence in video games just as there has been about violence on TV or violence in comics. The worry is that playing violent video games weakens the membrane between the reality IRL (in real life) and the reality of gameplay and therefore will increase the violence being acted out. There is now sufficient research to repudiate that notion.

We have violence in many forms today, as we always have throughout the history of humanity. Today we have wars, mass shootings, road rage, and domestic violence. Violence is built into our human nature, although most of us can restrain the actions that come from violent impulses. Perhaps the issue is that we do not have a truthful relationship with violence and that is one of the reasons it shows up in our movies, comics, and video games. We would like to overcome and eliminate violence, but we cannot. We must relate to it as an integral part of our nature. It is an abhorrent thought to most of us to recognize the contradictory nature of what we are, or as Jung would say, what lives in and through us. In essence, this is one of the messages in Jung's *Answer to Job*,[7] that the psyche is dangerous and unconscious of itself. Jung put it as God being unconscious of himself.

Video Games as Art

Video games, like other forms of contemporary art, show the culture what it is. Art is like a collective dream. It pictures what isn't seen or needs to be seen. Art often shows us what is being left out of conscious perspective, like a dream, is a compensation for contemporary collective consciousness.[8] Art is also avant-garde. Marshal McLuhan wrote, "Art at its most significant is a Distant Early Warning System that can always be relied upon to tell the old culture what is beginning to happen to it."[9]

Finishing *The Last of Us Part I* puts the gamer through a wrenching emotional experience. *Part II* increases the intensity as you play one character and then play against yourself as an opposing character. It takes you where you didn't know you needed to go—into a contradiction. Art may be beautiful and moving, but also be transgressive and disturbing. When it became available, I upgraded and bought a Play Station 5. The controller has even better haptics (sensations transmitted through the controller) than the PS4. When playing *Stray*, I enjoyed the feeling when the cat purred but was disgusted when attacked and eaten by the Zurks. My heart pounded as I raced to outrun the Zurks, mutant one-eyed creatures that had evolved from bacteria. I could feel the Sentinels shooting at me, and when they struck me, I, as the cat, died. It was unnerving.

That video gaming is art is confirmed by the fact that there have been notable exhibitions of video games in prominent museums such as the Smithsonian in Washington, DC, the Museum of Modern Art in NYC, and the Victoria and Albert Museum in London.[10]

Internal Structure of Video Games

When I thought about *The Last of Us* as a dream, I found useful what Jungian analyst Wolfgang Giegerich writes about the structure of dreams. Some can be like a fairytale, while others have the structure of a myth. Giegerich writes, "Fairytales are about a progressive development from an initial situation, such as a predicament, toward a final goal, the solution, that the story was headed for from the outset."[11] "Myths, on the other hand, show an action that only seemingly leads from here to there, but in reality merely unfolds the internal complex logic of one 'archetypal' soul moment or soul truth."[12] A myth is the unfolding, in narrative style, of one truth. A fairytale is a story of a beginning, a journey, to a conclusion. The internal structure is a fundamental difference between *Stray* and *The Last of Us*. *Stray*'s fairytale structure begins with an initial, undesirable situation and progresses to a final goal, opening the city. *The Last of Us*, while seemingly having a fairytale structure, has a myth structure where all aspects of the game are the unfolding of *one truth*: the world is self-decomposing. In Giegerich's terms, "soul is negating itself," meaning consciousness is negating itself as part of the process of the logic of negation and sublation, in order to bring it to a new form, a new status of consciousness. The current level of life, of consciousness, is already dead or dying, so to speak, and the fungus has come to fold it under and bring about a new life form.

In addition to his understanding of the inner structure of dreams, Giegerich stresses the importance of including resistance in dreams, especially one in which the dream ego is resisting the movement of the dream. This inner tension, the opposition, is the life of many dreams. He writes,

> The dream-I *has every right to his or her resistance* to the imposition by the "soul" as its host or master. The analyst's task is not to be against the dream-I's resistance or fight the patient's resistance. The resistance *is* part of the dream as a self, part of the whole picture, and the whole picture is just right, just as it is.[13]

Resistance is part of the process of change. One cannot just give in to the changes that are happening. In *The Last of Us*, the people fight for their lives against those infected by the cordyceps fungus. There would be no game if they didn't, and there would be no change without putting up a fight to resist the forces of change. Just as I joked about Stray becoming a "sublated" cat, an analogous change happens to Joel and Ellie, the humans who fight to survive and make it to the end. They are different people, changed by all the experiences they have gone through. The gamer, too, is changed by the experience, the hours of playing, being defeated, being killed over and over, and playing to the very end, perplexed and full of questions.

Of course, people (and cats!) don't become sublated, consciousness becomes sublated only after hundreds of years. Gradually the syntax of consciousness changes. Joel and Ellie represent the current status of consciousness and rightfully, from their perspective, fight the movement represented by the cordyceps fungus. That's why the ending doesn't matter. It isn't personal. It is the same whether Joel allows Ellie to die or saves her. There is no evidence that Joel didn't believe the vaccine would work, or that he wanted only to save Ellie, but there seemed to be a hint that he was skeptical of the whole procedure. Donating some of her blood in the attempt to make a vaccine was one thing. Sacrificing her life, was another.

Most post-apocalyptic stories have to do with survival, with the restoration of the "before times." Not *The Last of Us*. Something else is going on. Late in life, Jung anticipated something of the sort in a letter to Herbert Read: "Who is the awe-inspiring guest who knocks at our door portentously? Fear precedes him, showing that ultimate values already flow toward him. Our hitherto believed values decay accordingly, and our only certainty is that the new world will be something different from what we were used to."[14] The "awe-inspiring guest" in *The Last of Us* is the cordyceps fungus. A dictum from *The Last of Us*, "Endure and survive!" is a proper post-apocalyptic saying that contrasts with the anodyne saying of Mr. Spock from the 1960s *Star Trek*, "Live long and prosper." We live in an "endure and survive" era that is a genuine paradox. Collectively speaking, enormous changes are happening, most of which we are unable to understand.

The "Arcane Substance" at Home

Before I began to play video games, changes were happening at home. While retaining the outward structure, the internal structure of my marital relationship began to crumble. My spouse stopped working and retreated inward during which time he slowly abdicated his usual partner tasks, obligations, and companionship. My alarm at this was joined with anger and fear. What was happening? Was he ill or depressed or just choosing not to take the garbage and recycling out on Sunday night? Was he forgetting what day it was? He became refractory when asked about other usual tasks. When will you take the car in for servicing? "I'll take care of it!" But he never does because he forgets, or does he? The resistance that replaced his usual cooperation was perplexing. Becoming angry on my part made matters worse. He became quietly obdurate. His attitude became "I'll do exactly what I want to do," which turned into sleeping a good part of every day. I wake him up, and perhaps he will get up, have a little breakfast, and then return to bed. I was furious! But mostly I was terrified that something terrible process was happening to him with disastrous consequences for me. No doctors. He didn't go to any doctors anymore. Besides, all the ones he liked had died or retired. His best friends had all died and any kind of work was unthinkable. I thought he was depressed, but he claimed he was not depressed, did not feel ill nor did he feel anxious. "I feel slow," he sometimes said. "I think about my dead friends," he would offer when queried. I thought with dread of Alzheimer's.

I discovered bills were not being paid on time, if at all, and his supplemental health insurance had lapsed months ago, so long ago that it could not easily be reinstated. He was not the responsible man I had known only a year ago. Gradually, I took over all the finances, cancelled his credit cards, and spent many hours with an insurance broker to reinstate his health insurance.

I was in a state of intense anxiety, at the loss of my partner, an unusual mind, smart, highly intuitive, curious about many things, and early on who taught me how to look at a photograph or a piece of art. He had been a collector of many things. Many years ago, he brought home a huge table lamp that looked monstrous and felt like an unwanted intrusion in the house. I hated it and I hated having to deal with it. However, I slowly came to see its wonder and it became a treasured item in my home office.

At first, playing video games became a distraction, a way not to think about what was happening. Later, playing video games became a solace and recluse for me each night as I struggled with the tension of emotions roiling in me. Finding success in containing my emotional turmoil became the same as success at getting my tabby cat, *Stray*, past a section of the bloodthirsty Zurks or the scanning Sentinels. My overwhelming anxiety and resentment became emotions to struggle with and overcome. "Endure and survive" became a personal motto for me. Often, I would boil it down to this day, "Endure and survive *this* day. Tomorrow will be its own thing." I would go to bed each night exhausted but having found some equilibrium.

Neither forward nor backward worked. Forward meant that I fight and try to force him to do something—maybe—with a great expenditure of energy, resulting in bad feelings between us. Backward meant to abdicate and let him do whatever or not, but the resentment, anger, frustration, and helplessness did not dissipate, no matter how I tried. In the state of "there is no choice, and any choice is not a good choice," I gave myself over first to completing *Stray*, which took many hours over many weeks. I felt guilty ignoring him each evening, but he claimed he did not mind, and that it did not bother him. I believed him. He always supported me in doing what I wanted to do. It was our custom that we allowed each other freedom to be who we are and pursue our interests and activities apart from each other. His interest was in sleeping, mine in playing *Stray* or *The Last of Us*. I was enthralled by those games for many months.

My mood of anger, resentment, and expectations grew and hung over the house. This made him withdraw even more. But he deserved it! Or did he? I could not discern whether he was willfully refractory or if he was doing the best he could. In either or in both cases, why should he live in the toxic environment of my sulky, petulant, resentful moods, and most of all, the feeling of my constant pressing agenda for him? My expectations, even my projections, my preferring to live with a partner involved in the world with stories to tell when he came home from work or from having read the daily newspapers. My agendas had to go, for both of us. Whatever was going on with him, early dementia, or aging willfulness, the thought that he deserves a loving presence gradually began to take precedence.

Playing my video games, and being obsessed with them, was integral to the change that began to happen. An "arcane substance" emerged: my thinking, feeling, and approach to him reoriented and recalibrated. I found ways to have fun with him and coax him into being more active mentally and physically. I restrained my expectations. He tries to do things and sometimes will get them wrong. Picking up food to go, it will be with a side of French fries rather than a salad. I protest, "But I never get French fries, always a salad." "Oh, well," he tries to explain. "I guess I told her *I* wanted French fries." I say, "It doesn't matter, anyway, I make salads all the time." Many things don't matter anymore.

Toward the end of *The Last of Us Part I*, the gamer becomes Ellie rather than Joel, who has been wounded and lies gravely ill in an abandoned house. Ellie takes Joel's rifle and goes hunting. She kills a rabbit and then notes that as sustenance, it will not last long. When she spots a deer, she goes for it. As the player, I was unable to use the bow and arrow needed to bring down the deer and move the game along. I had never learned to be skilled with the bow and arrow as I would have if I had found the bow early in the game playing as Joel. I was stuck. My arrows pooped out and plopped down, landing too short, ineffective except in frightening the deer and making it run off. Night after night I persevered and finally gave up. "Maybe I won't ever finish this game," I wondered to myself, "because I didn't get the bow earlier in the game." It was hopeless. I felt chagrinned and a bit stupid. I was stuck in my attitude. I felt shut down in myself, and grumbly. Once again, I felt lonely and sorry for myself. I was in a first-class quagmire of self-pity.

A few days later, *The Last of Us* called to me. I was determined to move past this part of the game and get to the next challenging part. Combing the Internet, I discovered I was incorrectly operating the bow and arrow. There it was. The correct way, and once I returned to the game, the deer was quickly disposed of, and I was back fighting the "infected" and killing the "clickers." I was exhilarated, and at the same time, I renewed my commitment to the changes happening within me.

I wondered about my prior discouragement and my thought of giving up finishing the game. Maybe I'd lost interest. The novelty had worn off. I had better things to do. The feeling of those thoughts was familiar. Giving up, giving in, settling, a constriction of possibility. Then the other side appears as a determination to find a way. I described this curious contradiction to my spouse, one evening, who remarked, "It's because you have an old brain. A teenage gamer would just keep playing at the problem." He was right. I get trapped in my mind that can too easily give up and settle into known patterns of thinking. A young person's brain is quick at experimenting and will persevere until it finds the solution. I cannot regrow the facility of a young brain, but I can be aware of my tendency to replay old patterns of giving up too easily and shutting down myself and my energy.

Likewise, I would repeatedly get stuck in a situation with my spouse, feeling discouraged, angry, and helpless. "You have to go see the eye doctor." "No, my eyes are okay. I see fine." "You don't see fine. It's been seven years since you had them checked. I am worried about your driving." I make an appointment for him. I remind him of the appointment, and he reminds me that his eyes are "okay, he sees fine, and doesn't need to go." I gently insist and reassure him that I will go with him. We go to the appointment and the nice lady ophthalmologist firmly but kindly tells him that he needs glasses to continue driving.

Frequently I first collapse into discouragement, anger, and worry with each new situation. It takes time to find a renewed determination to stretch my brain and figure out a way to deal with a new challenge. I am energized by each success. There is a dialectical movement both within my video game and within my marital relationship. There is always a new conundrum, a new problem. I must discover how "to use the bow and arrow" for *this* new challenge whether in the video game or in my relationship.

There is an oppositional tension between where I am forced to go—and my resistance. Oh, I had forgotten about the role of resistance! Early in this process, I angrily confided to a close friend, "I can't stand it. I want to divorce him." That was not a possibility, I knew, but it was a relief to express it. The gradual undoing of myself, my resistance to going along with it, watching how the two are in a dialectic,[15] one negating the other. That's how things move along.

I feel angry or sorry for myself but then find the "arcane substance" hidden within my situation. Like freeing Mercurius from matter, I am within a dialectic that moves me. And there is a secret happiness in being moved along by this process to which I have submitted and committed. I remember that Hillman and Giegerich wrote that inner tension is part of the dream dynamic.[16] Thinking about *The Last of Us* as a dream, now in my marital situation, resistance is integral to the dream process. *I fight what is happening to me in order to get where I am going.* I think and feel that I hate this situation, but it is taking me where I need to go.

Always tempting to think that *he* is the problem, I can feel that he is not the real problem. My spouse "is the outward occasion for an inner dialectic," a paraphrase from Jung who in describing God's tirade at Job wrote, "Job is no more than the outward occasion for an inward process of dialectic in God."[17] With the clarity of that thought, I find ways to make the situation work. There are practical issues to manage, and, in the future, there may be very difficult practical issues.

Recently, I played the penultimate section of *The Last of Us* in which Ellie gets tangled up with a group of cannibal survivalists with a sadistic leader named David. Toward the end of this part, Ellie must sneak up on David to injure and ultimately kill him. It is a challenging section even when I am playing on the "easy setting." As Ellie, I was killed many times with a machete by the vicious David. When I was able to succeed and finally kill David, I felt triumphant as if I had finished the entire game. I had not, as there was one last section of the game to get through. But it was a milestone for sure.

Correspondingly, I finally faced the facts I wanted to deny. I checked my spouse's symptoms on several websites and discovered that he clearly and definitively has MCI, mild cognitive impairment. This condition of mental confusion and memory loss can last for years, get gradually worse, or be the prelude to Alzheimer's disease. I felt relief in knowing that he wasn't and isn't just being lazy or difficult. He really is doing the best he can, and maybe then some. My expectations for him eased to yet another level and my warmth toward him increased as he accomplishes the things he still can do.

Penultimate

The "arcane substance" takes me to a different consciousness. It reaches me, happens to me, and allows me to think and feel differently. I am composting on the inside. I am a myth that is unfolding; my orientation and ruling dominants are being overturned and folded under. My daily and weekly tasks are goal-driven like a fairytale, like Stray getting past the Zurks or Joel escaping from the runners and the clickers. The larger unfolding of my life is to allow this "unwanted guest" to gain legitimacy in my life. For me to recognize what has come, unbidden to radically change me. To become a different version of myself. To become a sublated version of myself.

Notes

1 Naughty Dog, "The Last of Us, Part II," Sony Interactive, 2020.
2 Mike Isaac and Conor Dougherty, "Two Gamers Played 'The Last of Us Part II:' They Were Blown Away," *New York Times*, June 19, 2020.
3 Naughty Dog, "The Last of Us, Part 1," Sony Interactive, 2013.
4 Blue Twelve Studio, "Stray Video Game," Annapurna Interactive, 2022.
5 Todd Martens, "'Stray' Videogame Argues That Sci-Fi Dystopia Is Better with Cats," *Los Angeles Times*, July 19, 2022.
6 Louie Schwartzberg, *Fantastic Fungi*, Film, 2019.
7 Jung, *Answer to Job*, CW 11.
8 Jung, *The Spirit in Man, Art, and Literature*, CW 15, 122.
9 Marshall McLuhan, *Understanding Media: The Extensions of Man*, 1st MIT Press ed. (Cambridge, MA: MIT Press, 1994).
10 Julian Lucas, "The Puzzle of Putting Video Games in a Museum," *New Yorker*, June 30, 2023.
11 Wolfgang Giegerich, *Working With Dreams: Initiation Into the Soul's Speaking About Itself* (London and New York: Routledge, 2021), 138.
12 Giegerich, *Dreams*, 138.
13 Giegerich, *Dreams*, 145.
14 Jung, *Letters*, Bollingen Series, 95: 1–2 (Princeton, NJ: Princeton University Press, 1973), 590.
15 Hegelian dialectic is where the contradiction is found *within* the subject, which then negates the subject. A second negation brings about the *sublation*, a higher level of comprehension.
16 Giegerich, *Dreams*, 109.
17 Jung, *Answer to Job*, CW 11, para. 587.

Index

For Product Safety Concerns and Information please contact our EU
representative GPSR@taylorandfrancis.com
Taylor & Francis Verlag GmbH, Kaufingerstraße 24, 80331 München, Germany

9781032561257

This deeply personal book contains essays and articles that portray the evolution of the author as a practicing Jungian analyst. Themes of illness, death, and violence are inherent within the chapters of this book. She uses metaphors from music to describe transitions, some involve literal death, and others are metaphorical.

The chapters of this book provide an engaging and readable review of life from one Jungian psychoanalyst, featuring essays on topics such as physical illness, film, music, video games, and her dog. The author covers problematic psychological and physical conditions, each of which, through exploration and inquiry, provides a transition to a new depth of understanding and a renewed sense of self. The book begins with the death of Power's Jungian analyst and the subsequent experiences when she began a "new analysis." She describes a "mysterious illness" that took her from being a classical musician to becoming a Jungian analyst. Other chapters include one on the nature of violence, another on the clinical issue of the "negative coniunctio" in the consulting room, and another on body symptoms and illness as "vanishing mediators" that take her from one status to another.

A personal and engaging read, this new collection by an experienced analyst will be of interest to Jungian analysts, clinicians in both analytical psychology and psychoanalysis, and those undertaking psychoanalytic training.

Pamela J. Power is a clinical psychologist and Jungian psychoanalyst living in Santa Monica, CA, USA. She is a member of the C. G. Jung Institute of Los Angeles, where she served as clinic director and director of training. She has lectured nationally and internationally in the field of analytical psychology on a variety of topics. She is also a member of the Inter-regional Society of Jungian Analysts, the International Association for Analytical Psychology, and the International Society for Psychology as the Discipline of Interiority.

ANALYTICAL PSYCHOLOGY

an **informa** business

Routledge
Taylor & Francis Group
www.routledge.com

CERTIFIED
CARBON
NEUTRAL®
publication
CarbonNeutral.com

ISBN 978-1-032-56125-7

9 781032 561257

Routledge titles are available as eBook editions in a range of digital formats

Ken Fuchsman

Sigmund Freud's Inner Divisions

Personal and Theoretical

HISTORY OF PSYCHOANALYSIS
Series editor: Peter L. Rudnytsky

"It is a delight to travel with Ken Fuchsman as he insightfully engages with Sigmund Freud, both the man and the thinker. Fuchsman shows how Freud's internal struggles and conflicts produced contradictions, reversals, and lacunae in his theories. Any reader, no matter how familiar with the creator of psychoanalysis, will come away from this consistently arresting exploration with a renewed appreciation of Freud's contributions and a deeper sense of where and how Freud went wrong."

James W. Anderson, *PhD, Professor of Clinical Psychiatry*
and Behavioral Sciences at Northwestern University,
former president of the Chicago Psychoanalytic Society

"In this book, Dr Ken Fuchsman examines Sigmund Freud's self-analysis and his relationship with his father. After claiming that his father Jakob had sexually abused his siblings, Sigmund Freud retracted his statements and considered these facts as 'childhood fantasies'. The theoretical elaboration then saw fantasies take precedence over reality and fathers exonerated. It is the theoretical consequences on psychoanalysis of what looks like a denial of reality that Dr. Fuchsman examines brilliantly. Let us also remember that Sophocles, in the tragedy of Oedipus Rex that Sigmund Freud chooses as a reference, obscures one of the elements of the many versions of the Oedipus myth, namely the rape committed by Laios on the young Chrysippos, hence the curse that followed…"

Brigitte Demeure, *PhD in History, Master in Intercultural Studies,*
former vice-president of the A2IP (Association Internaitonale
Interactions de la Psychanlyse) and president of the
French Society of Psychohistory

"Ken Fuchsman, an eminent psychohistorian, has written a compelling and wide ranging book on Freud highlighting the relationship between Freud's inner conflicts and his theoretical project. The Freud of this book is one who wrestles with his own divided allegiances, which spilled over into his conceptual confusions, the fragmentary nature of his ideas, and internal contradictions in his writings. While Fuchsman sees Freud as an innovative, original, and deep thinker in Western intellectual history, praising him as someone who modified and changed his ideas throughout his long lifetime, the Freud of this volume is conceptually confused, whose ideas are often incoherent, and who often contradicted himself. As a skeptic, and as neither a devotee nor basher of Freud, Fuchsman views the father of psychoanalysis as limited and rather unscientific in developing the foundations of psychoanalysis. He is particularly good at deconstructing Freud's evolution from rebellious son to authoritative (and authoritarian father), from liberal to conservative, and from someone committed to empirical aspects of psychoanalytic methodology to one in his late period who was dogmatic and intolerant of criticism and dissent. Fuchsman has rewarding commentary on the Oedipus complex, the death instinct, paternal authority, the scientific status of psychoanalysis, and the role of splits in the history of psychoanalysis, many of which he attributes to Freud's inner conflicts and to unresolved ambivalences in his personality. Freud, of course, was an initiator of discourse on the role of psycho-sexuality, early childhood development, the role of the internal struggle between consciousness and the unconscious, the untamable nature of desire, and the lifelong struggle for recognition and mutual recognition. Fuchsman has an excellent command of the secondary literature on Freud (a kind of industry), and an astute but critical approach to Freud's primary texts. I can recommend this volume to students of Freud, to psychohistorians, and to mental health professionals who may not have a grasp of the personal origins of many of Freud's significant ideas."

David James Fisher, *Ph.D. is a psychoanalyst in practice for 46 years. He is a Senior Faculty Member at the New Center for Psychoanalysis and a member of the Board of Directors. He is also a Training and Supervising Analyst at the Institute of Contemporary Psychoanalysis in Los Angeles. His writings work at the intersection of cultural history and the history of psychoanalysis. He has published four books. The Subversive Edge of Psychoanalysis was published by Routledge in 2025*